A HISTORY OF
ENGLISH LITERATURE

A HISTORY OF
ENGLISH LITERATURE

BY ARTHUR COMPTON-RICKETT

GYAN

Published by

GYAN

Gyan Publishing House
5, Ansari Road
Daryaganj, New Delhi-110002
Phone: 011-47034999, 9811692060
E-mail: books@gyanbooks.com

Distribution Network
gyanbooks.com
India, USA, Canada, UK, Australia

ISBN: 978-93-6208-256-5 (HB)
First Published, 1912

2nd Impression 2024

Printed at: Gyan Press, Delhi.

A HISTORY OF ENGLISH LITERATURE
Author: ARTHUR COMPTON-RICKETT

A HISTORY OF
ENGLISH LITERATURE

By ARTHUR COMPTON-RICKETT, M.A., LL.D.

LONDON: T. C. & E. C. JACK
67 LONG ACRE, W.C., AND EDINBURGH
NEW YORK: DODGE PUBLISHING CO.

CONTENTS

CHRONOLOGICAL SYNOPSIS

I

THE MAKING OF THE ENGLISH SPEECH

THE ANGLO-SAXON PERIOD

(c. 670—c. 1050)

THE MIDDLE ENGLISH PERIOD

(c. 1050—c. 1400)

II

THE ENGLISH RENASCENCE

(1400–1660)

III

THE AGE OF SATIRE

(From Butler to Pope)

(*c.* 1660–1740)

IV

THE AGE OF SENSE AND SENSIBILITY

(*c.* 1740–1780)

V

THE ROMANTIC REVIVAL

(*c.* 1780-1832)

VI

THE VICTORIAN ERA

(*c.* 1832–1900)

A HISTORY OF ENGLISH LITERATURE

I

THE MAKING OF THE ENGLISH SPEECH

Introduction.—The fabric of our literature is shot with the varying tints of racial characteristics; the sombre imagination of the Celt, the flaming passion of the Saxon, the golden gaiety of France, and the prismatic fancy of the South. Many have been the influences brought to bear upon our speech. Yet in this composite texture the Anglo-Saxon element dominates. That is the outstanding fact. We have only to take some passage of modern poetry, say a few lines from Tennyson's *Passing of Arthur*, to realise clearly the complex character of our tongue, and the persistence of the Saxon element—

> "Then from the dawn it seemed there came, but faint
> As from beyond the limit of the world,
> Like the last echo born of a great cry,
> Sounds, as if some fair city were one voice
> Around a king returning from his wars."

Here we have in the ancient story of Arthur the earliest strand in our literature—the Celtic element; though the legend of the Mysterious Passing was interwoven with it at a later date by the French Romancers.

Looking at the words, forty-three in number, it will be seen that of these thirty-three are of Anglo-Saxon origin. For instance: dawn, from Anglo-Saxon *dagian*, "to become day"; king, from Anglo-Saxon *cyning*. This illustrates the practical predominance of the Saxon element in our speech. Of the remaining words, five are from the French—*e.g.* faint from old

French *faint*, and cry from *crier;* sounds from old French *soun;* city from French *cité*, and voice from old French *vois;* limit is from the French and Latin (*limite*, and *limes*); and echo is from the Latin and Greek (L. *ēcho*, and Gr. *ēchō*).

The passage quoted was selected at random, and some would have yielded a richer supply of words of French and classical origin; but this serves its purpose in indicating the French, and the classical (Latin and Greek) influences upon our tongue. One other point there is to note, namely, the persistence down to the present day of the old Saxon trick of alliteration. It is certainly less marked here than in many passages of Tennyson, but it is seen in such a line as—

> "*S*ounds a*s* if *s*ome fair city . . ."

The first thing to recognise in mediæval literature, is that it falls naturally into two periods—

(1) THE ANGLO-SAXON PERIOD, and (2) THE MIDDLE ENGLISH PERIOD. The first period (*c.* 670–*c.* 1050) deals with the legendary literature of an ancient Northern people. The second (1050–1400) with the experimental literature of a composite race.

What we have of the first is only a fragment, but for five hundred years it was a vital force in the lives of our Teutonic forefathers. And while the British were living under the easy surveillance of Rome, English literature was growing up in Scandinavia and Northern Germany, where the Angles and Saxons lived. So that when these Northern tribes came down upon our coasts, and after stubborn resistance drove back the British into a corner of Britain, they brought with them a poetry from which we may fairly date our national literature. This poetry is expressed in a language derived from old German. The British, or Celtic inhabitants were not exterminated; but persisted, and their legends (Welsh and Gælic) exerted later a powerful influence over the English. Then from the eleventh to the fourteenth century France dominated the literature of Europe, and England like other nations fell under her sway. This is the Middle English Period.

The Nature of Anglo-Saxon Poetry.—Anglo-Saxon poetry is markedly different from the poetry of the next period, for it deals with the traditions of an older world, and expresses another temperament and way of living; it breathes the influence of the wind and storm-wrack. It is the poetry of a stern and passionate people, concerned with the primal things of life, moody, melancholy, and fierce, yet with great capacity for endurance and fidelity. With the next period, a more vivacious, more romantic[1] element passes into our verse.

THE ANGLO-SAXON PERIOD

English Poetry before the Conquest of Britain.—The earliest English poem, written by our ancestors while on the Continent, is *Widsith—The Song of the Traveller*, a kind of travel journal, where the vagrant minstrel tells us of the people he has visited and places to which he has been. Another of these poems, *Deor's Complaint*, is a lyrical cry of one bard about another and more successful rival. This poem is probably our first English lyric.

The lyric, however, was not congenial to the English temperament; the epic, or narrative poem dealing with heroic deeds, being far better suited to his muse. Of such, *Beowulf* is the most representative.

Beowulf.—This poem of over 3000 lines has for its background Scandinavian scenery. It concerns a Scandinavian thane who comes to the help of his neighbour Hrothgar, and Beowulf tells us of his exploits, especially of his desperate fight with a terrible dragon, Grendel, possibly symbolic of the sea, to whose poison he ultimately succumbs, not however before killing the monster. The historical background is drawn with clear actuality, and the character of Beowulf is pictured for us vigorously and impressively. There is an Homeric greatness about the atmosphere of the poem, which makes it of real value to us in understanding something of the spirit of our Teutonic ancestors; it is certainly one of the most important monuments of Anglo-Saxon literature, and was found during the eighteenth century in a MS. written in Saxon times. Originally it was Pagan in tone, with the stern and dignified paganism of the old Sagas; but attempts were made in the eighth century to accommodate it (with ill success) to the faith of the day. The ideal of life it presents is a primal and strenuous one. Of the sentiment and tenderness dear to the later French romances there is not a trace. It deals with hard fighting, and hearty eating and drinking, tells of the delight of music after the toil of the day; of

[1] The term *romance* originally meant a tale in verse written in a Romance dialect—Latin. It was concerned with wonderful adventures, and its secondary meaning has usurped its original signification. But the tenour of the Romance differs from the Epic, also concerned with stirring exploits, in its emphatically sentimental character.

full-blooded elemental passion, and carries that undernote of fierce regret on the brevity of life and the certainty of death, so characteristic of Northern poetry.

But its interest goes beyond this, for it paints, simply and clearly, the social customs of our ancestors—how they lived in peace and war; what their town and country places looked like; of their attitude towards their women folk; of their pleasures and their hardships.

And what we may gather about our ancestors is this:

Anglo-Saxon Life.—The Anglo-Saxons were a pastoral people, living on the fringe of the Baltic and the North Sea, in a country bleak and low-lying; though not unfitted to cradle a brave and hardy race. Tillers of the soil, and hunters by compulsion, they became also by force of circumstance fierce sea-rovers. Inured by long privation to the terrors of the sea, they made little of its dangers, and a Roman writer has told us, how that they would plunder the western coasts, sailing down upon them in their high-prowed warships in the midst of a storm so that their victims might be the less prepared. Truly enough were they likened to sea-wolves.

In appearance they were big, large-limbed men, with blue-grey eyes and ruddy of face; relentless, savage and daring, yet courageous and faithful to one another, and among their women folk gentle and loyal. Above all, law-abiding according to their lights, and with that fierce passion for independence that has always marked our race. The freeman had his house with its long hall, where he ate and slept with his comrades, on the straw-strewn floor. The women kept house, spinning and weaving garments for the men, while the men folk roved abroad. Yet they also took part in public affairs; shared in all social functions; held property, and in the open-air assembly or moot, helped to settle local affairs. In social life among the Greeks, as described by Homer, we have a very similar picture of the way of living; and as with the Greeks, so among the Saxons, was there a Minstrel or Glee-man in each household, who sang songs at the close of the day—songs of ancient tradition mingled with verse of his own making.

English Poetry after the Conquest of Britain.—So far, the poetry, though written in the English language, is not part of the literature of England. The first native English maker of verse is Cædmon.

CÆDMON.—The aged herdsman, Cædmon, so Bede tells us, put into verse stories from the Bible in the lonely monastery of Hild that stood on the rough moorland near Whitby, overlooking the German Ocean. And his verse-making came about on this wise.

Leaving the feast and the singers, because he could not take part, he fell asleep among the cattle. And while he slept he dreamed that one came to him and commanded him to sing. "Of what am I to sing?" said Cædmon. "About the beginning of created things." He then fashioned a song about the Creation, and awakened from his dream. The song he remembered, and made many more like it. And after this he became a monk.

These stories in verse—*Cædmon's Paraphrase*—were written about 670, and became very famous. Thus did the old paganism merge into the Christian sentiment of the time. Of these poems only a fragment has survived, quoted by Bede and carried from monastery to monastery. But the influence of Cædmon upon his successors was great. The religious note in English verse, persisted throughout the Middle Ages, died down at the Renascence, but reappeared again in Milton, and continued until Victorian times.

CYNEWULF.—Cynewulf, his successor, is full of the new religious ardour. Writing about the close of the eighth century, he sings of "the clashing of the sea waves," and "the rolling of the waters" and of "foaming billows" that cover the earth; but his verse has nothing of the old pagan wistfulness. It is alert and joyous.

During the following century the scattered poems of the past were gathered together into collections, and in the tenth century religious poetry is mingled with plentiful war songs, such as the *Song of Brunanburgh* (937), where the conflict between Saxon and Dane figures prominently.

Characteristics of Anglo-Saxon Poetry:—

1. It resembles Hebrew poetry, indulging in parallelism[1] and metaphorical phrases.

2. In metre it is marked by accent and persistent alliteration.

3. Rhyme is absent, and there are no definite number of syllables. The metre undergoes a good many variations, and responds to the nature of the subject.

4. The poetry was sung, for in early times poetry and music were one and indivisible, and the minstrel was free to modify the movement of the verse. Any modification introduced was,

[1] By *parallelism* is meant the repetition of the same *statement* or *idea* in different ways; by *alliteration* the repetition of the same *letter* at the beginning or in the body of different words, in close juxtaposition to one another.

however, subject to certain rules. There were always four accented syllables and three alliterative syllables. Many changes were wrought later in the Middle English period through French influences, but the trick of alliteration has become an integral part of all English poetry; and though no longer a structural part of English prosody, is regarded to-day as an ornament, not an essential. It has been used with most remarkable effect by Swinburne.

5. There is a prevalence of compound words, by means of which the poet sought to condense the qualities of his subject. This characteristic also has survived.

For instance, when Rossetti speaks of "hoarse-tongued fire," or Keats of "leaden-eyed despair," they are using a poetical method derived from our earliest verse.

6. The style of this poetry is, on the whole, diffuse, though when the writer is greatly moved it becomes more simple and direct. And while there is force and vigour, and often the austere splendour of the Icelandic Saga about the work, there are no graces or subtleties, and the lyric note is extremely rare.

The form of poetry chiefly favoured by these elder writers is the epic; it suited both their manner and matter, and lent itself to the treatment of heroic deeds. William Morris's translation of the Scandinavian Sagas will give the modern reader a fair idea of the trend and character of this early poetry.

Anglo-Saxon Prose.—The prose, unlike the poetry, was not used as an emotional stimulant. It was in the main educational.

BEDE is the first name we encounter here. Like Cædmon he was a Northumbrian, with a passion for learning only equalled by his piety and fidelity to his monastic order. He studied eagerly every department of human thought—the philosophies, arts, and sciences: and to his *Ecclesiastical History* we are indebted for our knowledge of the England of his time. He wrote in Latin for the most part, but was quick to recognise the possibilities of the Saxon tongue, and when dying is said to have repeated to himself some of these old poems.

Northumbria marked the centre of the earlier Saxon literature. With the coming of the Danes in the tenth century the seat of scholarship and study passed to Wessex.

ALFRED.—Alfred is the next influence with which to reckon. He is a real founder of English prose, just as Cædmon is the originator of its poetry. He wrote in English, not in Latin, and used it to teach history, politics, religion, to the people. During his reign the *Anglo-Saxon Chronicle* came into existence; and if not his own work, it probably owed much to his inspiration. This is the most important landmark of Anglo-Saxon prose, and continued beyond the Conquest down to the death of Stephen.

EDGAR AND ELFRIC.—Under Edgar and Elfric prose literature continued to flourish, and to become stronger and more varied in expression.

But the Danish invasions made great inroads upon the progress of literature during later Saxon times, though it was far too vital a thing now to be suppressed.

Characteristics.—At its best, as in the fighting episodes of the *Anglo-Saxon Chronicle*, Old English prose is clear and forcible, and occasionally, in the hands of Elfric, rhythmic and musical. But it is well to remember that its chief aim was that of instruction, and for the most part religious in nature, concerning itself with the stories of the Bible and the lives of the Saints.

THE MIDDLE ENGLISH PERIOD: POETRY AND PROSE

Latin was the language in which the cultured man of Norman times wrote, and French was the language spoken in polite society. The Saxon tongue languished, and there is little doubt that the Norman Conquest did for a time militate against the development of our literature. Many Saxons wrote in French, and, with the exception of the *Saxon Chronicle*, which went on until 1154, the bulk of the prose was written in Latin. English prose after the *Chronicle* practically slumbered until its remarkable awakening in the sixteenth century.

Yet, after all, the Norman Conquest was not the conquest of England by an alien race. The Normans were originally Northmen like the Anglo-Saxons and Danes, even though southern influences had greatly modified their character and outlook. And this affinity was ultimately felt by both Saxon and Norman. Consequently there was a real fusion between the two races. On the Saxon side we accepted the traditions of France in matters poetical. On the Norman side we finally chose the Saxon tongue in place of the French in which to express ourselves.

Middle English Poetry.—The old Saxon verse, with its sober dignity and strong religious bias, abruptly ceases after the Conquest. But this is less the result of the Conquest than the effect of the dominance of French poetry throughout Europe. The old alliterative verse indeed had declined before the Conquest, becoming a negligible quality until the fourteenth century, when there is a most extraordinary revival, the *Morte* *d'Arthur* and *Piers Plowman* being two of the most famous examples. In the twelfth century even the Scandinavian peoples took from the French their ballads and rhymings. The successful fight with the French in the twelfth and thirteenth centuries helped to consolidate both the English people and their literature. And in the reign of Edward I, English poetry once again became a force. It has, however, changed in character.

Let us examine the new medium of expression. On the one side it retains an elder characteristic, the religious note; on the other side it presents a new phase, the romantic note, derived from France.

(a) *The Religious Note.*—The scholastic activities of the twelfth and thirteenth centuries favoured the continuance of religious verse. Those ripe scholars, Lanfranc and Anselm, were the early inspirers, and later on the missionary monks sent by Bernard of Clairvaux further stimulated devotional verse.

Orm's *Ormulum* (*c.* 1215), a metrical version of the Gospels with some hortatory matter added, is the first of any importance. The sources of this book are the old Saxon writers, Elfric and Bede. Following this come Lives of the Saints in verse; English Saints being given special prominence—*e.g.* St. Cuthbert, St. Dunstan, St. Swithin, St. Wulfstan. In addition to the verse there are pious treatises in prose; one, for instance, the *Ancren Riwle*, or rule for recluse women (Anchoresses), which belongs to the thirteenth century. This is an ascetic manual for young women who wish to dedicate themselves to God. The author, Bishop Poor of Salisbury, preaches the gospel of self-abnegation, yet in a conciliatory and gracious manner. But he will have no paltering with worldly things. Domestic pets must be restricted to one cat, and the young women must refrain even from glancing out of the parlour windows.

The teaching of religious doctrine by means of verse and prose proceeded with great vigour under the Mendicant Friars; and it was necessary to give it in a palatable story form in order to interest the people. A notable book of this kind is the *Cursor Mundi*, written about 132), which treats in poetical form of the historical portions of the Bible, with a number of legends about Saints in addition. Like the early Mysteries and Miracle Plays, it was a means of popularising, clearly and vividly, sacred story.

In all this work there is abundance of French words, and practically no alliteration. The language is in a transitional stage.

The greatest religious poem of the time, *The Book of Piers the Plowman*, must be given more detailed consideration.

WILLIAM LANGLAND and his *Book.*—Probably of low

extraction, Langland was from his earliest years familiar with the poor folk both of the city and of the country.

His mental alertness had interested others in him, and of patrons he had not a few. But after a while these died, leaving him to look out for himself. We find him living in Cornhill, poor and unhappy, with his wife Catherine and daughter Nicolette. Too old to form fresh friendships—he had never been a companionable man—he strides the streets with bitterness in his heart.

True, he had one solace—his book—and one feels that into it was poured his life-blood; all his hopes and despairs, his sorrows and aspirations, his anger and his compassion went into these Visions.

Like another famous writer of allegory, he fell asleep, and in a "field ful of folkes" he saw the men and women of his dream—knights, monks, preachers, peasants, cooks that cry out "Hote pyes hote," and "mystrelles" that sell "glee." And the object of their journey, like that of the more famous journey from the City of Destruction, was the search for Truth and Good.

He reproaches—

> "Bochiers and cokes [1]
> For these are men on this molde
> That most harm wercheth [2]
> To the pooere people
> That percelmale briggen [3]
> For they empoisone the people
> Priveliche and ofte." [4]

Also he condemns the rich people for "regrating"—that was the custom of buying up provisions and retailing them to the poor at great profit.

In his ethical earnestness and sombre outlook he had a forerunner in Richard Rolle, a Yorkshire hermit and mystic, who wrote in the Saxon tongue, both verse and prose, to benefit the common people.

Langland, though the spokesman for the labouring classes, favoured the old class divisions and reviled the insurgents of 1381; in these matters he is reactionary. He wants reform, but within the Church. He is less drastic in his proposals for clerical reform than Wyclif.

For instance, the knaves who traffic in "pardons"; the friars who make a pretence of religion; knights to whom fighting

[1] Butchers and cooks.
[2] Worketh.
[3] Piecemeal bring.
[4] Privately and often.

was merely an excuse to express their lust for blood; the countless men and women, both in town and country, whose lives were dominated by no great principle or ideal—all these he lashed; the rottenness, which was breaking up all the real strength and greatness of the Middle Ages, Langland saw with marvellous clearness. Where can truth be found? This is his cry. And so the messengers—Reason, Repentance, and Hope—help in the search for truth, guided by Piers himself. Piers insists upon manual labour as the first essential, and extols this with the enthusiasm of a Thoreau.

The World is at hand to wheedle and bribe the honest worker; the World in the person of Lady Meed, attractive but heartless, whose name itself savours of bribery.

Especially vivid is the picture of the revellers in the City Tavern. Here we have quarrels or discussions, and heavy drinking, and the noisy ritual of mirth for which taverns in every age are renowned; the hermit, the cobbler, the clerk of the Church, the hangman, and the harlot met together.

The scene shifts constantly and unexpectedly from town to country—from London to Malvern; vigorous and pungent homilies break in upon the action of the story, and the upshot of all is that the poet bids us "lerne to love" as the one cure for the ills of life.

With Langland, the special characteristic of the old Saxon verse, alliteration, long neglected, is used once more. The verse is rough and uncouth, but is passionately sincere.

The *Visions* were very popular, and soon became the spoken symbol of the suffering poor. JOHN BALL invokes his authority, and even so late as the Reformation, the name of Piers is in use. He stands for the "ideal" working man.

Along with Langland we associate naturally WYCLIF, for there was the stuff of the religious and social reformer in each, though Wyclif's outlook was the wider and clearer. A hard-headed and keen-witted Yorkshireman with a vigorous spirit of independence, he soon took part in the ecclesiastical disputes of the age. Championing the cause of the common people, he set the authority of the Bible against the authority of the Church; and in order to familiarise the people with the Bible he started, with others, the translation of the Bible into the Saxon vernacular, reinforcing its teaching with sermons and tracts of his own, written in simple and homely speech. His importance in the history of English prose is rather as the chief translator of the Bible than as an independent writer, for in the latter capacity his work is often too heavily burdened with Latinized terminology. English prose lagged far behind poetry in its vital development; for until the fifteenth century it was used but very rarely except for educational purposes.

(b) *The Romantic Note.*—In religious poetry we were carrying on, if in a somewhat altered fashion, the traditions of Saxon literature. But romance is a new departure altogether; it was something alien to the Saxon genius.

The elements of sentiment and gaiety are brought for the first time into English literature. Dignity, passion, force—these things are indigenous to Saxon poetry; to them is added the graceful sentiment, the light and shade, the volubility of Norman verse.

Roughly speaking, it is possible to differentiate this romantic poetry into "courtly" and "popular"; meaning by courtly the poetry that grew up around the Court, and expressed itself in a chivalric ideal—*e.g.* the Arthurian tales: and by popular, the poetry that centred round familiar country festivals, such as the May games—*e.g.* the Ballad. The courtly poetry scarcely emerges into great distinctiveness, however, until the time of Chaucer; though there is a constant striving in that direction during the two preceding centuries.

French poetry had in it these two elements—the courtly and the popular, and they quickly attached themselves to our national standards of thought. It is not always possible, however, to distinguish the two, for there is that famous duologue in verse—*The Owl and the Nightingale*—by Nicholas de Guildford, in which the courtly and popular elements are inextricably blended.

Now, in the French Romantic poetry, which came over here and so profoundly influenced our literature, there were three important story-cycles: the matter of Rome, the matter of France, and the matter of Britain.

The first includes the story of Troy, and the adventures of Alexander of Macedon. The Trojan story inspired Virgil, and was popular in France during the twelfth and thirteenth centuries. More than one nation fancied descent from Pius Æneas, in an age when to have descended from some fabulous person was looked upon as a guarantee of national respectability. The Greeks themselves claimed Trojan origin, and Geoffrey of Monmouth in his *History of the Britons* described with gusto and particularity their descent from Brutus, great-grandson of Æneas.

The first notable English Poem after the Conquest.—Curiously enough this tale, which greatly took the popular fancy, was translated into French, and re-translated later on by the priest Layamon under the title of *Le Brut* (1205). A striking feature about Layamon's work is the introduction of rhyme into English verse in parts of his work, and the use of similes.

The adventures of Alexander had found an earlier ingress, but there are very few English poems dealing with it, though Chaucer says that everyone had heard of Alexander's fortunes.

The matter of France is more important as a literary influence. It dealt with Charlemagne, and started in France with the *Story of Roland*. The groundwork of this cycle is historical, and the struggles depicted between the feudal nobles and their over-lord are based on fact; though such a hero as Huon de Bordeaux is a figment of the imagination.

This cycle was wonderfully popular in mediæval times, and greatly influenced European literature—for example, the stories of Ariosto. In our own time William Morris drew upon its romantic treasures.

This cycle reached its height of development in the eleventh century. It appealed to the Southern nations more than to us, because it was concerned so particularly with the struggle of Christendom and Mohammedanism.

The matter of Britain is, for Englishmen at any rate, by far the most important of these cycles.

What was it?

It was a cycle of stories, of French origin, written partly in prose, partly in verse, dealing with the old Celtic legend of King Arthur. We are so accustomed to regard Arthur as a national hero, that we do not realise readily how largely the literature around him is in a foreign tongue. For the height of its popularity in the twelfth and thirteenth centuries was the height also of French influence And it was in the form of a French Romance that the stories became known in England.

It is somewhat curious that we should have adopted as our national hero the chief of the defeated Britons rather than a Saxon leader. But such is the fact; other epic heroes we passed aside, and took to our hearts the Celtic conqueror of the "Demon Cat."

We do not know what precisely was the character of the original Welsh legend, but we do know that it was mainly concerned with fighting, and that the Launcelot story and the legend of the Grail, together with other tales of King Arthur's knights, were after-thoughts—French embroideries on to the original theme.

Sir Thomas Malory later on blended the Arthurian literature —prose and verse—into one prose version.

So much for the chief romantic matter of the Middle Ages. Other romantic poems of interest to the student of English literature are those around Sir Gawain—one of King Arthur's knights, *Pearl*—in which the romantic and religious notes merge into an elegy of grief for a personal loss; and English versions of Norman romances, such as *Havelok the Dane*, *Guy of Warwick*, *Bevis of Hampton*.

These, like Welsh Geoffrey's *Brut*, were English or Danish in origin, and had travelled back again to England viâ France.

Ballad Poetry.—Most compelling in its interest is the rich store of ballad poetry, wild flowers of English verse, that had grown up during the Middle Ages, and were, in the fifteenth century, snatched from the country-side and garnered in at the bookshops of Westminster.

The charm of the ballad lies in its naïve simplicity and primitive feeling. To call it artless, as some do, is a mistake, for it has its own rules of diction, its tricks of phrasing, and conventional refrains. But it has the ease and sincerity of genuine poetry, and is deep-rooted in its love of Earth and primal human qualities. Such a line as this would have thrilled Scott:

"And the birk and the broom blooms bonnie"—

And there is the poignancy of Burns in the cry of Margaret to her dead lover in *Clerk Saunders:*

"Is there ony room at your head, Saunders?
  Is there ony room at your feet?
Is there ony room at your side, Saunders?
  Where fain, fain I wad sleep."

Homely pathos, old time magic, a fierce love of independence, and a brooding sense of tragedy—these are the things that meet us in such pieces as *The Nut-Brown Maid*, *Chevy Chace*, *The Bonny Earl of Murray;* while the love of outdoor life and the changing seasons meet us in the Robin Hood ballads, and such lyrics as the well-known "Sumer is icumen in, Lhude sing cuccu."

The term ballad is used to cover a wide variety of verse, but the word originally signified a dance-song;[1] and many ballads eloquent of love, youth, and the springtide were sung

[1] From *ballare*, to dance.

by the villagers at their feasting times to a rhythmic measure.

What we have are the product of Saxon intensity of feeling, softened and lightened by Norman sentiment and grace; though the ballad measure is of ancient origin, and probably dates from early mediæval times.

Early History and Philosophy.—If Geoffrey of Monmouth is the popular historian of the age, William of Malmesbury is the scholarly one. His account of the kings of England is marked by scrupulous care in dealing with ascertained facts, eschewing fantastic legends. Glanville and Bracton contribute to the making of constitutional law; the former from the practical, the latter from the theoretical standpoint. Roger Bacon, a Franciscan Friar, is one of the earliest scientists, and in a frankly unscientific and credulous age is noted for the insistence he laid upon the supreme value of experiment.

Gower and Chaucer.—Contemporary literary judgments are seldom of value. Ben Jonson was rated by his age above Shakespeare, and his own generation failed to appreciate Milton. So we need not be surprised to find Chaucer's friend, John Gower, placed on a higher pedestal than the author of *The Canterbury Tales.*

Later judgments have perhaps unduly depreciated Gower. He was a writer of much talent, and his important poem, the *Confessio Amantis* (*c.* 1393), by its sweeping and varied collection of mediæval tales, certainly prepared the way for Chaucer. It is very useful pioneer work. His inferiority to Chaucer is shown in the uncertain way in which he uses the vernacular, still preferring on the whole the "polite" tongue of the day—French.

Chaucer.—*The Man and his Career.*—Geoffrey Chaucer, born of the merchant class, spent his early life in London, by the Walbrook stream; and at seventeen he was appointed page to the wife of Lionel, son of Edward III. In this way he gained acquaintance with Court life and manners. After a military expedition to France in 1359, which led to his capture by the French and subsequent ransom for sixteen pounds by Edward, he became first a personal attendant of the King; later on a squire. He saturated himself in the French Romances—notably the *Roman de la Rose*—and promptly and naturally imitated them. In 1370 Chaucer travelled abroad in the King's service, to Flanders, France and Italy—to the Italy of Giotto, Petrarch, and Boccaccio; in short, to the world of the early Renascence. Need we be surprised that the sojourn in Italy profoundly impressed the imagination of the English poet. Hitherto he had been ignorant of Italian literature; now he reads the great writers, and the glamour of the *Roman de la Rose* fades away.

Not one but many are the visits paid to Italy, and in the meantime we find Chaucer fulfilling the prosaic duties of Comptroller of Customs at Aldgate; living much as Hawthorne lived his consular life at Liverpool, a business and practical man on one side, and a dreamer of dreams on the other. It is at this time that he wrote *The Parliament of Foules* (1382), the translation of *Boethius*, *Troilus and Criseyde* (1382), *The House of Fame* (1384), and *The Legend of Good Women* (1385). And over them all is the magic of the South. But the Italian, like the French inspiration, begins to die away. The rich concrete qualities of the man begin to clamour for a more temperamental utterance, and during the closing years of the fourteenth century he gives us *The Canterbury Tales.* It is possible that Boccaccio's *Decameron* may have suggested the framework of the poem—the succession of story-tellers. But for the subject-matter the poet has gone directly to the life of his own day.

The Form of the Canterbury Tales.—Of this work about 17,000 lines are in verse, while two stories—the tale of *Melibeus* and the *Parson's* tale—are in prose. The verse consists of rhymed couplets. It forms a compromise between the old and new prosody. Chaucer does not care for alliteration or doggerel rhyme, and chooses the form of "heroic" verse, with rhymed couplets and five accented syllables.

The tales themselves are of astonishing variety. Some are drawn from the romances of chivalry—*e.g. The Knight's Tale.* Others deal with moralising scriptural stories—*e.g. The Monk's Tale.* Some are fine adaptations of romantic stories of ancient France. There are, between the stories, prologues, where Chaucer's gift of sharp and vivid characterisation is best seen—*e.g.* the *Discourse of the Wife of Bath.*

The Characterisation.—And when the prevailing tendency of the age to deal in allegory and abstractions is taken into consideration, it is astounding how alive these Chaucerian types are.

For in the course of his life he had come into contact with them all. The Knight, the Squire, the Merchant, the Sailor, Scholar, Doctor, Monk, Labourers, Saints and Knaves—he knew then intimately and drew them from personal observation. He knew the Court folk; he knew the People; and he draws them for us with all their little tricks and mannerisms and external peculiarities. We recognise one by the raucous tone of the voice, another by his rubicund face, another for her sensitiveness: she was so "pitous" she wept to see a mouse caught. We see the parchment face of the Knave, the jolly rubicund countenance of mine Host,—we become acquainted in a word with the mediæval Englishman as he moved and lived, depicted with a breadth of vision and a rich tolerant humour unsurpassed in our literature. The poignant note that we find in Langland is absent, for Chaucer takes rather the comedy view of life; but this must not be held to imply any lack of sympathy with the poor and suffering. There is a large-hearted charity in his treatment of the labouring class, as his picture of the Ploughman will testify.

And there is an open-air atmosphere about it all. His people are always on the move. Never do they become shadowy or lifeless. They shout and swear, and laugh and weep, interrupt the story-teller, pass compliments, and in general behave themselves as we might expect them to in the dramatic circumstances of the narrative. And it is never possible to confuse the story-teller; each is distinct and inimitable, whether it be the sermonising Pardoner, the hot-tempered Miller, or the exuberantly vivacious Wife of Bath, who has had five husbands, but experience teaching her that husbands are transient blessings, she has fixed her mind on a sixth!

There are tragedies as well as comedies in the Tales; some are grave and subdued, others ablaze with colour and merriment. But the thread of honest and kindly laughter runs through them all, serious and gay alike.

There is nothing of the dreamer about Chaucer—nothing of the stern moralist and social reformer. Like Shakespeare, he makes it his business in *The Canterbury Tales* to paint life as he sees it, and leaves others to draw the moral.

Langland's mordant pictures of contemporary life gave an actuality to poetical literature which removed it far from the old heroic stories with which the name of poet hitherto had been connected. And Chaucer realised what those who followed him for many years to come were too blind to see—that the genius of the English people did not lie in high-flown tales of sentiment, but in homely stories of everyday life, illumined by shrewd observation and tolerant humour, and occasional moralising.

And the crowning glory of *The Canterbury Tales* lies in the fact that in this masterpiece he uses "naked words in English." He has made the new language throb with life, and put the corner-stone on the edifice of English Mediæval Literature.

II

THE ENGLISH RENASCENCE (1400–1660)

In Italy and Germany a stirring of fresh life, a kindling of new desires, a spiritual expansion of human experience, were already potent influences. We call this wider outlook the Renascence, though each nation expressed it in its own way. In Italy it speaks through the senses; in Germany it becomes a moral message. The literary student may judge of the distinctive atmosphere of the two countries by reading the *Fra Lippo Lippi* and *Johannes Agricola* of Robert Browning. In England the spirit of the Renascence is more slowly felt, and not until the close of the fifteenth century can we find much sign of its influence.

While it is impossible to reduce this Renascence spirit to a cut and dried formula, it is possible to distinguish in it two leading inspirations. The one, the intellectual impulse resulting from the study of the classics. The other, the imaginative impulse given to men's minds by the geographical discoveries. It was the spiritual fusion between the old and the new world that gave birth to the Renascence—the old world of Greece and Rome, and the new world across the wide seas.

The Renascence in England is felt first of all then in educational centres, such as the Universities of Oxford and Cambridge; and its earlier exponents are earnest and strenuous scholars like Roger Ascham, Sir John Cheke, Nicholas Udall: men who regarded sober citizenship and moral worth as being of more account than graces of style and beauty of expression. But gradually, as the reading of ancient literature awoke a keen appreciation of the melody of language, and the adventurous spirit of the time warmed the imagination of Englishmen, we have the pulsing of a fresher and more vigorous life in our poetry and prose.

Meanwhile there is a transitional period in our literature, which is chiefly of significance to the student, as showing how the seeds were sown for the rich flowering time of the Elizabethan Age.

Chaucer's impecunious friend, Thomas Hoccleve, and John Lydgate, a monk at Bury, give us some vivid pictures of London life in their writings; and the uncouth figure of the Norfolk cleric, John Skelton, stands out as a doggerel writer of rude power, who helped to pave the way for the new poetry. But the freshest and most individual verse of the time comes from Scotland, where the national spirit had recently been kindled in an ardent flame by the hardly-acquired independence at Bannockburn.

Scottish Nature Poets.—John Barbour sings of Freedom, with all the passionate conviction of Shelley. James the First, a diligent student of Chaucer, has in the *Kingis Quhair*[1] given us in Chaucerian stanza work instinct with a genuine love of Nature, and a meditative charm not to be found in any of his contemporaries. After him the schoolmaster, Robert Henryson, may be remembered also for his description of Nature and vigorous morality. One of his best poems is quaintly entitled *Garment of Good Ladies.* Most remarkable of all are William Dunbar and Gavin Douglas. Douglas excelled in his description of Scottish scenery, Dunbar in his rough but genuine humour.

Turning from poetry to prose, there is nothing to note of first-class importance until we come to the work of CAXTON and SIR THOMAS MALORY'S *Morte d'Arthur.* This book is of special significance. Not only did it give unity and artistic form to the various and scattered legends of Arthurian Romance, but it introduced these stories to thousands who would never have come across them. Written in a prose style of simple rhythmic charm, it is a veritable delight to all lovers of Romance; and its persuasive magic has inspired some of the finest poets of our time.

From *The Paston Letters* (1422–1509), the chit-chat of a county family, we gather incidentally how considerable is the growth of interest in classical learning. The *Utopia* (1516) of SIR THOMAS MORE, written in Latin, supplies us with a wonderful picture of the effect of the Renascence spirit in stimulating the social ideals of thoughtful Englishmen. If to his book we add Lord Berner's translation of *Froissart* (1523-25), we cover the most remarkable products of the Transitional period.

We are on the eve of the English Renascence now—a time of imaginative splendour, which lasted with few fluctuations until the coming of Milton.

1. THE DRAMA

In a crude and clumsy form the Drama had existed long before the sixteenth century; the Elizabethan transformed it into a thing of force and beauty. Yet it is curious to find how

[1] *Quire*, or *book*.

poor an opinion the Elizabethan had of the dramatic art. Even Shakespeare, who considered carefully the publication of his poems, treated his dramatic scrip with careless contempt. The Play was something to be seen—not to be read. An appreciation of this fact explains to some extent the loose construction of many of the dramas, as well as the note of violence and coarseness so persistently struck. It was an age when bear-baiting and cock-fighting were favourite sports; when cruelty and bloodshed were a part of our ritual of mirth, and the Tower, "London's lasting shame," as Gray called it, dark with years and sinister with secrets, served as the symbol at once of despotic power and princely magnificence. Indeed, when we consider the character of the playgoers, and the persistent demand for horseplay and brutality, we can only marvel that the genius of our greater men—of Marlowe, Shakespeare, and Ben Jonson—rose so often superior to the demand of the moment. Not the least of our national debt to Shakespeare is due to the way in which he helped to widen our vision and mellow our sympathies. In an age which hated the Jew as an alien and moral monstrosity, he gave us a Shylock; and to a generation that revered above all the man of action, he gave a Hamlet.

Roughly speaking, it may be said that the Drama was born under the shadow of the Church and nurtured for religious purposes. The value of the spectacular appeal in an age when printing was unknown is of profound importance. And had not the Church fostered the Drama for her own purposes during the Middle Ages, it would not have been the force it was in the age of the Renascence.

First Stage in the Development of the Drama.—Obviously, Drama is inherent in the very ritual of the Church; for the Mass itself is a doctrinal point presented in spectacular form. In order to familiarise men and women with the stories of the Bible these were acted from time to time—the season of the year determining the nature of the play. Stories which were taken from the Bible were called *Mysteries;* those taken from the lives of the Saints, *Miracle Plays.*

Second Stage.—The second stage is reached when the play emerges from the Church into the market-place. This was effected when the Gilds were entrusted with the performances in the fourteenth century. It was customary for each craft to represent a play according to its particular trade. For instance, the Fishermen presented the Flood; the Vintners, the Marriage at Cana. The work was very seriously taken by the

Gilds, lack of competence and unpunctuality being met by heavy fines.

Performances were given on cars or scaffolds in the open spaces of the town. There was no attempt at scenery, but attention was given to stage properties. There was a monstrous head with movable jaws to represent Hell; and, in addition to a rich costume, the actor had some symbol to denote his part—*e.g.* St. Stephen had a stone; God was symbolised by the Papal dress.

The play of *Noah* gives us some insight into the nature of these plays, and shows the blending of rough English humour with didactic purpose. For though the drama had its source in sacred story, in the *method* of telling we can trace the influence of the old English amusements—the Pageants and May Games, the horse-play of the Juggler, and the quips of the Jester.

Noah having finished his Ark informs his wife of the fact, and begs her to enter. Dame Noah, however, having determined to go on a jaunt with a crony, declines the invitation with some finality of manner. After an altercation, in which the services of the son Japhet are enlisted, she is compelled to enter. But no sooner in than in a true shrewish spirit she boxes her husband's ears! And he finds, poor man, that although sheltered from one storm he has exposed himself to another.

On the whole, Miracle Plays proved more popular than Mysteries, probably on account of their fresher subject-matter. Each big town had its own Cycle of Plays—*e.g.* York, Chester, Coventry.

Third Stage.—The third stage is reached when the Mystery and Miracle Play give place to the Morality and Interlude. In the Mystery and Miracle, serious and comic elements were interwoven. Now they part: the Morality presenting the serious and the Interlude the lighter side of things. The Morality was frankly didactic, dealing in abstractions and allegory. The characters typified certain qualities—*e.g.* Sin, Grace, Repentance. The Interlude aimed merely at amusement. Famous examples of both types of play are found in *Everyman* and *The Four P's of Heywood.*[1]

Moralities continued to flourish up to the end of the sixteenth century, and were popular even in the heyday of Shakespeare's fame.

Fourth Stage.—The fourth stage sees the beginning of English tragedy; for Tragedy preceded Comedy, in England as in Greece. We have reached now the influence of the Renas-

[1] a *Pardoner*, a *Pedlar*, a *Palmer*, a *Poticary.*

cence, and see the effect of classical influences. Seneca's Tragedies, with their earnest and strenuous atmosphere, attracted the writers of the day; and *Gorboduc*, the first English drama, is the result. This was written by Sackville and Norton, and played before Elizabeth at Whitehall in 1562. When published it was called *Ferrex and Pollux*. Its intrinsic merits are slight, for it was frankly imitative, and its verse is stiff and lifeless. But the classical model served to give some form and coherence to the crude shapelessness of the drama at the time.

Of more importance at this period was the development of English Comedy, as exemplified by *Ralph Roister Doister* (*c.* 1566) and *Gammer Gurton's Needle* (1575), plays rich in English humour; the first (the better of the two) showing a keen sense of dramatic movement.

One thing is clear from these works, and that is the gradual approximation of the drama to the life of the day—especially the comedy side. There is real vitality, but so far little literary grace or power. This gift, however, was now to be bestowed.

The initial stages of this glorification are due to a new school that had arisen, called "The University Wits"—a professional set of literary men. Of this little constellation, Marlowe is the central sun, and round him revolved as minor stars Lyly, Greene, Peele, Lodge, and Nash.

Marlowe.—Christopher Marlowe was born in Canterbury of humble stock, and dreamed his early dreams in the cathedral city. Later on he went to London, where he varied his literary work with reckless bursts of dissipation, and died in an inglorious brawl at Deptford in 1593.

With little of Greene's power for actualising the life of the day, or Lodge's clear-cut characterisation, Marlowe had a wealth of poetry in him far transcending that of any contemporary save Shakespeare.

What did he do?

He raised both the matter and manner of the drama to a higher level. In the first place by seizing large, serious subjects for treatment, that appealed to the imagination; in the second place by turning blank verse, at his coming stiff and unyielding, into a thing of delicate and plastic beauty. Compare these lines from *Gorboduc*—

> "O hard and cruel hap, that thus assigned
> Unto so worthy a wight so wretched end;
> But most hard, cruel heart, that could consent
> To lend the hateful destinies that hand
> By which, alas, so heinous crime was wrought"—

with these from *Faustus*—

> "Was this the face that launched a thousand ships
> And burnt the topless towers of Ilium?
> Sweet Helen, make me immortal with a kiss.
>
> . . . . . .
>
> Oh, thou art fairer than the evening air
> Clad in the beauty of a thousand stars!"

How did he work this transformation?

He found blank verse consisting of lines, each ending with an accented monosyllable; each line standing nervelessly by itself. He modified the rhythmic pauses, changed the accents, made the metre suit the subject instead of fitting the subject to the metre, and in his own words bade farewell "to the jigging veins of rhyming mother-wits, and such conceits as clownage keeps in pay." Moreover, he gave, what the elder plays lacked, form and coherence to his subject.

His Plays.—*Tamburlaine.*—Tamburlaine is a Scythian peasant who becomes a mighty monarch, until at last, drunk with the blood of his enemies and his own insatiable ambition, he is smitten with sickness by the Gods.

Faustus.—Faustus, like Paracelsus, aspires to all knowledge, and sells his soul to gain it. The story here is of the Middle Ages, though Marlowe gave it a Renascence setting, transforming the anxious alchemist into an ardent idealist, and softening the material horrors of the mediæval version.

The Rich Jew of Malta.—This play lacks the pictorial splendour of *Tamburlaine*, and the imaginative beauty of *Faustus*, but has a superb opening scene, and presents a remarkable study of avaricious passion.

Edward II.—Edward II is on another plane entirely. It has nothing of the glitter and pomp of the earlier plays, but is incomparably better constructed, and shows more psychological power.

Marlowe saw clearly enough that the Romantic Drama was suited to the needs of the nation, and that therefore no other form of drama could express so well its abundant, concrete life. But he saw also that for the Romantic Drama to be a thing of beauty as well as a force, the medium of blank verse must be chosen. No finer tribute was paid him than that given by Michael Drayton, in *Epistles of Poets and Poesy* (1627):

> "Neat[1] Marlowe, bathèd in the Thespian springs,
> Had in him those brave translunary things

[1] Ingenuous.

That the first poets had: his raptures were
All air and fire which made his verses clear;
For that fair madness still he did retain
Which rightly should possess a poet's brain."

"Fair madness" is a satisfying phrase fit to rank beside the noble suggestion of Keats, that "Poetry should please by a fine excess."

He had, of course, the defects of the temperament of his age; a frequent over-luxuriance of imagination, a lack of restraint, an extravagance bordering on the ridiculous. But no criticism can obscure the greatness of his genius. He found the drama crude and chaotic; he left it a great force in English literature.

Marlowe's genius did not incline him much to the lyric, though his famous *Passionate Shepherd* shows what he could do in this direction. But his fragmentary narrative poem, *Hero and Leander*, has a fresh, sensitive beauty transcending the coarser magnificence of young Shakespeare's *Venus and Adonis.* The haunting line, "Who ever loved that loved not at first sight?" lingered long in Shakespeare's memory.

The other writers of Marlowe's group, though markedly inferior, must not be overlooked, for one and all contributed in some measure to the transformation of the drama, in which Marlowe was the chief factor. Lyly gave it literary grace, Peele informed blank verse with a sweetness and melody second only to that of Marlowe. Two of his most notable plays were the *Battle of Alcazar* and *David and Bathsheba:*

David. "Now comes my lover tripping like the roe
And brings my longings tangled in her hair,
To joy her love I'll build a kingly bower
Seated in hearing of a hundred streams."

The plays of Greene, Lodge, and Nash show less skill in the manipulation of blank verse, and less sustained beauty. On the other hand they have abundant vitality and vigour, and both Greene and Lodge were, of course, melodious and accomplished song writers.

Thomas Kyd followed the Senecan School very closely, and is largely responsible for the "blood and thunder" element in the Elizabethan drama. He ranks below his contemporaries in dramatic and poetic power. But he did his share in breaking away from the pedantic dullness of *Gorboduc.*

The Theatre.—The drama flourished for a considerable while before the theatre—council chambers, guild halls, the yards of inns, these being the theatres of the early Elizabethans. The

Queen had her Company of Players, and most of the noblemen theirs.

The first regular theatre was built at Blackfriars by James Burbage in 1576. Afterwards came the Curtain, in Shoreditch, 1576; the Globe, in Southwark—the famous "Wooden O," 1594; the Fortune, in Shoreditch, 1599. Performances took place daily in the early afternoon, and lasted for about a couple of hours. Shakespeare's plays were given only at Burbage's theatre and at the Globe.

These early theatres were large wooden sheds, partly thatched with rushes, a flagstaff on the roof, and surrounded by a trench. They clustered round the swampy ground beside the Thames, and gave rise to a good deal of vexation to quiet citizens in the neighbourhood. For around these playhouses in the afternoons the narrow, tortuous streets were so crowded by a noisy, frivolous concourse that "business suffered in the shops, processions and funerals were obstructed, and perpetual causes of complaint arose."

But despite objections by the residents and bitter criticism by the Puritans, theatres multiplied rapidly. In the majority of theatres the auditorium, as in ancient Greece, was open to the sky, only the stage being roofed. Thus the pleasure of sight-seeing was of a doubtful kind in bad weather.

There were no tickets. A penny (about fivepence in our money) admitted to standing room in the yard. Rich spectators watched the performance from boxes on each side of the stage, paying about twelve shillings in modern reckoning for the privilege of a seat. In the upper proscenium box were the orchestra of the Globe, the largest in London, composed of ten performers, with drum and trumpets for the martial scenes, oboes and flutes to suggest the sentimental passages.

The fashionable part of the house was on the stage itself. There sat the royal patrons of the theatre, Essex and Southampton, with their friends. Failing seats, these gentlemen sprawled upon the rush-strewn boards, over which they spread their rich cloaks. Here also sat the dramatic poets of the time, to whom were accorded a free pass. Most important of all to us were the shorthand writers, commissioned by piratical booksellers, who took down the dialogue, under pretence of criticising it, and thus preserved for posterity many plays that otherwise would have been lost.

The giving of a tragedy was signalised by draping the stage with black; for a comedy blue hangings were substituted. A placard hung upon one of the stage doors bore the legend of

Venice or Verona, as the case might be; no other indication was there of the *mise-en-scène*. In the battle scenes an entire army scurried in and out through a single door. One can understand the apology of the Prologue in *Henry V:*

> "Can this cockpit hold
> The vasty fields of France? or may we cram
> Within this wooden O the very casque
> That did affright the air at Agincourt?"

No women ever appeared on the stage, and few attended the theatre at all. It was far too rough a place, but the Queen summoned the players to Court on special festivals—Twelfth Night, and so on.

Shakespeare.—Born in 1564, at Stratford-on-Avon, the son of a well-to-do burgess, William Shakespeare came to London about 1587. His father's fortunes had declined, and his unhappy early marriage to Anne Hathaway, combined with the lack of employment, were instrumental probably in driving the youth from country lanes to the streets of London. Another factor in impelling him Londonwards may have been the visit of the Queen's Players in 1587, turning his thoughts stagewards. Be that as it may, to London he came, and in 1594 there is mention of him as belonging to the Lord Chamberlain's Company. Actor, re-shaper of old plays, poet, dramatist, and manager, such are the chief phases in his career. Little as we know about the facts of his life, we can gather that, together with extraordinary creative powers, he must have combined a shrewd and businesslike capacity for ordering his affairs.

In 1612 there is reason to suppose he returned to Stratford, and lived there with his daughter until 1616, when he died of a fever.

The period of Shakespeare's literary activity extends over twenty-four years (1588–1612), and this may be broken up into four sub-periods.

The First Period (1588-94).—Here historical plays predominate. He continues the work of Marlowe, and essays to mirror the broad national features of Plantagenet life. The one tragedy, *Romeo and Juliet* (1592), is essentially a young man's tragedy, strong in lyric beauty though lacking the grandeur and breadth of the later tragedies; while *The Merchant of Venice* (1594), though in form a comedy, is in a sombre framework of tragic irony, relieved by a golden thread of romance.

For the rest, he writes in buoyant spirits a social extravaganza, *Love's Labour's Lost* (1591); a rollicking farce, *The Comedy of Errors* (1592); a sentimental romance, *Two Gentlemen of Verona* (1591); and a fantastic romance, *A Midsummer Night's Dream* (1594–95).

Marlowe probably had a share in the *Henry VI* plays; he frankly inspired *Richard III* and *Richard II; King John* being the first of the historical plays which shows an emergence from the domination of Marlowe.

THE SECOND PERIOD (1594-1600).—Shakespeare has now found himself. There are three historical plays here, finer in quality than those preceding, the two plays of *Henry IV* (1597) and *Henry V* (1598). *Henry V* is the more showy, and has been well described as a "National Anthem in five acts"; but the *Henry IV* plays are far richer in humour and psychological power. Of the comedies, *The Taming of the Shrew* (1595) and *The Merry Wives of Windsor* (1598) are cast in the early farcical vein, though the handling is easier and stronger; *Much Ado about Nothing* (1599) is on a higher plane of wit; while in *As You Like It* (1600) and *Twelfth Night* (1600), humour and romance blend in perfect proportion.

To this period belong the Sonnets, printed later in 1609. There are two series, the first addressed to a young man, one to whom Shakespeare had been deeply attached; the second concern a woman, one who has obviously played the part of an evil genius in the poet's life. For simple intensity of feeling and variety of expression, they are, as love sonnets, unrivalled in our language.

THE THIRD PERIOD (1600–08).—In the third period Tragedy predominates, and we reach here the culminating point of Shakespeare's power as a dramatist. The romances of the period, *All's Well that Ends Well* (1595), *Measure for Measure* (1604), and *Troilus and Cressida* (1603), are essentially tragedies set in a key of forced comedy; they are rich in poetry, but leave a confused and unpleasant impression upon the mind.

Incomparably greater are the Tragedies. Starting in grave measured style with *Julius Cæsar* (1608), he rises to greater heights of drama and reflective poetry in *Hamlet* (1602); while in *Othello* (1604), *King Lear* (1605), and *Macbeth* (1606)—that superb trilogy of plays, imaginative subtlety and passionate intensity make of these dramas the most superb and compelling in our literature.

THE FOURTH PERIOD (1608–12).—The last period opens with Tragedy. *Antony and Cleopatra* (1608), with weaker dramatic grip than its immediate predecessors, but fully as ripe in the strength of its characterisation. *Coriolanus* (1609), *Timon of*

Athens (1608), and *Pericles* (1608), are only fitfully great; but when in the eventide of his career he turned again to his first love, Romance, we get *Cymbeline* (1610), *The Tempest* (1611), and *The Winter's Tale* (1611).

The tragic period has left behind it a legacy of spiritual power and imaginative subtlety which make the last works of the dramatist a fitting pæan of farewell.

Nature of the Shakespearean Drama.—In Shakespearean drama almost every phase of the life of the age is mirrored, from the particular craze and fashion of the moment to the broad, general characteristics of the national life.

Thus *Love's Labour's Lost* (1591) was in its inception a social satire dealing with the fashions and fads of the day. Euphuism[1] and extravagance in dress are derided with as much topicality of allusion as a play of Bernard Shaw would show to-day. The Elizabethan pedant figures amusingly in Holofernes, who has been "at a great feast of languages and stolen the scraps." Hotspur's speeches abound in reference to current fashions—*e.g.* he speaks of velvet guards on the dress of fashionable city ladies, and there are many references in the plays to favourite games and sports —*e.g.* the mention of tennis in *Henry V.*

And just as he deals with ephemeral fads and crazes and some passing event, so does he deal on a much larger scale with the broad phases of Elizabethan national life. The dull-witted country constable is held up for ridicule in *Love's Labour's Lost* and *Much Ado about Nothing.* The elaborate ritual of Court life is depicted in *A Midsummer Night's Dream* and *Antony and Cleopatra*; its trickeries and pretentiousness in *Hamlet, Timon of Athens*, and *Cymbeline.*

How clearly is reflected in the plays the whole-hearted belief of the people at large in good and bad spirits. Hamlet asks the Ghost:

> "Be thou a spirit of health or goblin damned—
> Bring with thee airs from heaven or blasts from hell?"

And *Macbeth* is set in a similar background of witchcraft. Or to illustrate from his romantic plays—the fairy beings in the wood near Athens, the spirits that obeyed the behests of Prospero, were, we may be sure, as real to many of Shakespeare's audiences as Helena and Miranda.

In all of these matters Shakespeare was of his age. That is the Elizabethan side of him. An astute borrower, with a ready eye for a good plot wherever he might chance to find it; a

[1] See *post*, page 52.

skilful reader of the pulse of the public; a gentle, sensitive, sensuous and somewhat melancholy man; often called upon, against the grain we may conjecture, to satisfy the rough taste of the "groundlings."

But there is the universal side of the man. He was of his age; but he was also of the ages. And this by virtue, not so much of his dramatic power, which often suffers through the loose texture of his work, but of his incomparable poetry and insight into human nature. He is the supreme poet in an age of great poetry, because his poetry is wider in range and deeper in feeling than that of his contemporaries. He touches every mood: of graceful sentiment, as in the romantic comedies; of delicate fantasy, as in the fairy plays; of philosophic meditation, as in the tragedies of the mid-period; and of poignant passion, as in the later tragedies. In the verse that bodies forth such primal things as love, hate, hope, despair, courage, endurance, Shakespeare towers above his fellows. And when we think of Lear in his desolation, of Othello in his last anguish, of Macbeth in his soul agony, and the despair of Cleopatra—we think of English literature at its grandest.

Of his insight into character, it may be said that a ready test of the actuality of his characters is the impression they make on the modern reader. Portia, Rosalind, Beatrice, Cleopatra, Juliet, are startlingly modern. Placed beside the women of Sheridan or Goldsmith, and you realise how the latter are dated and how alive and fresh are the former. Beside them even the women of Dickens and Thackeray seem old-fashioned. And the reason is that Shakespeare's women have the primal qualities of womanhood common to every age, and therefore can never be dated.

And there is subtlety no less than actuality. Are not the nervous breakdowns of Richard III and Macbeth, the contrary moods of Cleopatra, indicated with rare delicacy of effect? With what masterly touches the figure of rash, hot-tempered Harry Percy is drawn. How impatient he is about the medical advice on the field of battle:

"... He made me mad
To see him shine so brisk and smell so sweet,
And talk so like a waiting gentlewoman:
Of guns and drums and wounds—God save the mark!—
And telling me, the sovereign'st thing on earth
Was parmaceti for an inward bruise!"

While with unerring insight Shakespeare differentiates such

vital rogues as Falstaff, the Tavern haunter, and Autolycus, the Vagabond of the fields.

Ben Jonson.—*The Man.*—A clever boy at Westminster School, probably of Scottish origin, who attracted the attention of Camden the historian; a bricklayer who studied Juvenal and Horace while plastering walls, a soldier in Flanders, a duellist, an actor, a poet, a playwright—such is a brief summary of Jonson's career. Personally a tall, stalwart man, hearty in his likes and dislikes as in his eating and drinking; satirical yet affectionate; domineering yet free from jealousy—sincere, direct, brave, quarrelsome—such a man was "rare Ben Jonson."

His methods.—Unlike his contemporary Marlowe, he is largely a maker of comedy. Unlike Shakespeare, he is content to satirise men and women rather than to present them in their entirety. He is a moralist in the first place, artist afterwards. But his scope is very wide, comprehending tragedy (*Sejanus* (1603), *Catiline* (1611)), masques, comedies, farces. Under James I he was literary dictator, the leading spirit at the "Mermaid" Tavern, numbering among his friends Shakespeare, Beaumont and Fletcher, Chapman, Herrick, Camden, and Bacon.

His technical skill.—At the outset of his career he refurbished old plays in the romantic manner; but this ill-suited him. Shakespeare when manager helped him at a critical point in his career by staging his comedy, *Every Man in his Humour*—where not only the individual anti-romantic note is clearly struck, but his skill in construction is first seen. Perhaps the best example of his dramatic construction is in the comedy of *Volpone*, where Jonson exposes the vice of cupidity with relentless but finely sustained satire. Dryden looked upon this play as the most admirably constructed specimen of modern dramatic art. But another comedy, technically almost as satisfying as *Volpone*, is *The Silent Woman*, where a number of intrigues are blended with rare skill, and the interest steadily accumulates from scene to scene.

With all his admiration of Shakespeare, Jonson disliked the easy-going selection of plots dear to his great contemporary. His advice to younger dramatists on this point is certainly sound, for he reprehends those who "waylay all the old books they can hear of, in print or otherwise, to fare their scenes withal . . . as if their imagination lived wholly upon another man's treacle."

Detailed observation.—There is no more elaborate painter of London life than Jonson. Shakespeare paints with a bigger brush; but for detailed effects Jonson is supreme. He satirizes vice with the vigour of Molière, but not with his adroitness. Had he lashed less furiously he might have kept a better edge on his rapier. Truly did a friend once say to him, "You write with a porcupine quill dipped into too much gall."

Yet this over emphasis was certainly not due to any blunted observation. His similes are neat and happy. For instance, this of an ill-bred man:

> "He minds
> A curtesy no more than London Bridge
> Which arch was mended last."

And when he keeps his didacticism in check, as in that amusing farce, *Bartholomew Fair*, his observant humour finds abundant scope.

Zeal of the Land Busy abhors Fairs and all their vanities, but is discovered "fast by the teeth in the cold turmey pie . . . with a great white loaf on his left hand and glass of Malmsey on his right." Later on he moralises (*à la* Pecksniff at Todger's) about his food. "We may be religious in the midst of the profane, so it be eaten with a reformed mouth."

His graceful fancy.—In imaginative intensity Jonson is inferior not only to Shakespeare, but to Marlowe, Webster, Beaumont and Fletcher, and other contemporaries. But he had a graceful fancy which showed to rich advantage in the Masques; and here and there it lightens up the Comedies with luminous flashes.

His last work, *The Sad Shepherd*, contains some of his pleasantest conceits. The shepherd laments his charming Earine; spring had died with her, and since then earth has borne but thorns:

> "Here she was wont to go, and here, and here,
> Just where those daisies, pinks, and violets grow:
> The world may find the spring by following her . . ."

His lyrics have sweetness and abundant grace. As instances, there are the songs, "O do not wanton with those eyes," the "Celia" cycle, and the familiar paraphrase from Philistrates, "Drink to me only . . ."

His mind and imagination never fused with the white heat of creative passion, as was the case with Shakespeare, but he exercised a wholesome effect on the drama where Romanticism had been carried too far.

This indifference to form, this careless exuberance of treatment, mattered little in the hands of Shakespeare. Instinct there often took the place of rules and conventions. But Shakespeare's method could found no school, and imitation of him led to disaster.

The more deliberate observation of Jonson, his adherence to classical conventions, his careful scholarship, his insistence upon a clear appreciation of what the writer wished to express—all these matters were of serious importance to writers who had talent but no genius.

The influence of Jonson lasted well on into the eighteenth century.

Of the crowd of dramatists who succeeded Shakespeare and Ben Jonson, it is impossible to speak save in the briefest fashion. A few of them, Beaumont and Fletcher, and Thomas Heywood for instance, were more voluminous than even Jonson. Heywood boasted that he had had "an entire hand, or at least a finger" in two hundred and twenty plays. Small wonder that with this productiveness few of the plays bear to be read except in snatches. They were for the most part hurriedly produced to meet the continual demand for fresh drama; and were composed frankly to please an audience, not to interest the student.

But around this crowd of names a few detach themselves by virtue of special qualities, and at the head are Beaumont and Fletcher. Marston and Tourneur are more passionate, Webster more poignantly tragic; Dekker has greater gaiety, Thomas Middleton a more brilliant wit. But for a combination of these characteristics in some measure, Beaumont and Fletcher take the palm. And in one quality they certainly excel their contemporaries—artistic restraint.

The weakness in the majority is the insistence on what is merely horrible and obscene. This is something other than the hearty coarseness of Shakespeare; it is the trick by which a writer seeks to gain preference over his fellows.

Among the most remarkable of these dramas are: (1) for gaiety and vivacity and insight into contemporary Life, Beaumont and Fletcher's *Knight of the Burning Pestle*—*The Spanish Curate*—*The Wild Goose Chase* (an Elizabethan version of *Man and Superman*); Middleton's *Changeling*, and Dekker's *Shoemaker's Holiday;* (2) for tragic intensity, Ford's *Broken Heart*, and Webster's *White Devil*, which is superior to his more conventionally pathetic *Duchess of Malfi*.

Towards the historical drama Chapman (the translator of Homer) and Heywood did good work. And in the development of the comedy of manners developed later by the Restoration dramatists, Massinger in his *New Way to Pay Old*

Debts (1633) played an important part. He is the forerunner of the brilliant satires of the Restoration drama.

2. Poetry

Elizabethan poetry has all the freshness and vigour of youthful race—

> "Bliss was it in that dawn to be alive,
> But to be young was very Heaven."

At first the poets—scholars and courtiers—could do little but stammer with fitful grace. The instrument is there, but they cannot as yet pipe on it. They are embarrassed and self-conscious. But this awkwardness melts away. When we reach Spenser and Sidney, the tentative flutings are over. The music is sweet, spontaneous, full-throated.

And so abundant was the output of poetry, that when the drama had taken all it needed, there was a wealth of melody left over.

The poetry of the age opens with the publication of a volume known as *Tottel's Miscellany* (1557).[1] This book contained the verse of those ill-fated courtiers, Sir Thomas Wyatt and the Earl of Surrey, and marks the first English poetry of the Renascence.

Of these two names Wyatt's is the more important. Modelling his work upon Italian models, he attempted a great variety of metrical experiments—songs, madrigals, sonnets, elegies; somewhat imitative, but with touches of grace and fantasy.

Surrey is seen rather as the disciple of Wyatt than an independent force; though at times his sonnets are more effective than those of Wyatt. Wyatt adhered strictly to the Petrarcan model, used with such fine effect at a later date by Milton, and still more recently by Rossetti. Surrey modified the form, and it was this modification that Shakespeare seized upon in his splendid Sonnet sequence. The Petrarcan form is perhaps the more impressive; the modified English form the more expressive.

Surrey also translated the second Æneid into blank verse. *This is the first example of blank verse in English.* Rhymed verse hitherto had held undisputed sway; but one effect of the study of the classics was to lesson the prestige of rhyme.

[1] Richard Tottel, a printer who, along with Grimald, a University scholar and chaplain to Ridley, made a collection of verse written by courtiers of Henry VII.

Surrey's blank verse was very unlike the sonorous measure it became in the hands of Marlowe. But it was a step at any rate in the direction of a form of literature in which the greatest Elizabethans won their highest triumphs. Surrey and Wyatt stand in relation to the glory of English poetry under Spenser and Shakespeare as Thomson and Collins do to Wordsworth and Shelley.

Gascoigne, like most of the earlier verse-writers, was a man of breeding and good education. His blank verse is more vigorous than Surrey's, and there is a greater individuality in his lyrics—*Flowers, Herbs, and Weeds* (1575).

Thomas Sackville strikes an even stronger note. Here at last we begin to escape from the stiffness that cramps his immediate predecessors. There is real music in his verse; and *The Complaint of Buckinghame* shows both variety and power of pathos.

But there is as yet little indication of that exuberant delight in life afterwards so manifest.

Surrey is inclined to dwell on the little miseries of love; Gascoigne is largely concerned with sorrow and the underworld; and Sackville's fancy is quaint rather than ardent, pensive, not joyful.

In fact, the Elizabethan poet, so far, is like Romeo in his early stage of love for Rosaline, which was more or less of a fancy to be embellished with literary tears and sighs.

SIR PHILIP SIDNEY, one of the most attractive personalities of the time, strikes a richer and deeper note. Cultured, sensitive, witty and ardent, he spent many years of his life in travel. But in 1578 he settled down in London, and for about ten years, until the time of his death, he devoted himself to literature.

Less brilliant than Marlowe, less witty than Lyly, inferior to Spenser in glamour, and excelled by many a contemporary songwriter in deftness of fancy, he has produced a body of work which for its versatile excellence places him in the foremost rank of his time.

Of his *Arcadia* and its remarkable influence, mention is made elsewhere. Here may be noted the discerning critique—*The Defence of Poesy*—where he uttered those poignant simple words that go to the root of all poetry: "I never heard the old story of Percy and Douglas, that I found not my heart moved more than with a trumpet."

And his quick and sensitive imagination enables him to pluck out the very soul of song. "It is not riming and versing that maketh a poet, no more than a long gowne maketh an advocate, who tho' he pleaded in armour should be an advocate and no soldier."

In poetry it is as a sonneteer that he will be best remembered. Out of his own disappointments in love he wove a fine cycle of sonnets to "Stella," some of remarkable sweetness :

> "Ring out your belles, let mourning sheaves be spread,
> For love is dead."

Edmund Spenser.—"An over-faint quietness"—wrote Sidney in 1581—"should seem to strew the house for poets."

Hitherto the scholar and courtier had ruled the domain of fantasy with pleasing and graceful, though not very vital results.

But from 1590 to 1600, Sidney's lament about the dearth of poetry dies down. The richness of the drama in those years has already been noticed; its fecundity in poetry was equally remarkable.

And Edmund Spenser is the forerunner of this great movement. He showed to Englishmen the music and beauty of his mother-tongue, as none since Chaucer had shown it.

In early years, along with the *Shepherd's Calendar*, are nine comedies on Italian models. The comedies have not survived, nor can we regret the fact. Certainly Spenser's talents did not point that way. He lacked the humour and actuality of his great predecessor ; and his muse was too wedded to allegory to interest herself in forms other than the Morality.

The Shepherd's Calendar is a medley of twelve pastorals on the months of the year. The form is one made fashionable by Virgil, though copied by him from the Alexandrian Greeks ; it was an artificial form of poetry approved by the age, and already taken advantage of by the accomplished Sidney in his *Arcadia*.

There is no real attempt to get at either the beauty or the homeliness of country life as we get it in Wordsworth or Crabbe. It is merely a peg for some robust moralising, and excellent fantasy, and satire.

But *The Shepherd's Calendar* pales in significance beside the *Faërie Queene*.

This poem was neither written in England nor inspired by England. Ireland is the inspiration ; Ireland is the scenic background ; Ireland supplies the stuff of adventure ; Ireland—the troublous, storm-tossed Ireland of Elizabeth's reign.

The enemies of Gloriana were flesh and blood enemies ; the knights came from Elizabeth's Court—were not Raleigh, Ormonde, and Grey of their number? And for this reason, perhaps, this poem has been called the Epic of the English Wars in Ireland under Elizabeth.

The poem reveals a sober, chaste, and sensitive spirit; one keenly alive to sensuous beauty, but kept from the grossness and coarseness of some of his brilliant contemporaries by a mind of singular refinement; and beauty is for him of the supremest value in life. Small wonder that Keats was fired by his verse, for certainly his famous phrase, "A thing of beauty is a joy for ever," is entirely Spenserean in sentiment.

The poem set out to be a story with twelve knights of Elizabeth who undertake various enterprises in her honour. But the poet had, unlike Chaucer, little gift of narrative, and soon wanders off the main road into the flowery meads of fancy. Starting in the middle of one of the adventures, he never completes his initial design, and the poem is merely a lovely mosaic into which are woven deeds of chivalry and pictorial fantasies, and grave moralising. From the pleasaunces and excitements of chivalry Spenser takes his ideas; yet he is not content merely to tell an entertaining story as Tasso and Ariosto had done, but to present his visions in a framework of high and noble purpose. Indeed, in a letter to Raleigh he avows his purpose is "to fashion a gentleman . . . in virtuous and gentle discipline."

What differentiates Spenser from, say, Shakespeare the poet, is the equable calm that pervades even his fervour. Sensitive to every phase of imagination and beauty, there is always a dreamy atmosphere about his verse. The sharp, vivid intensity of Shakespeare is not his; but he has his own particular charm. For an analogy to Shakespeare's poetry we must turn to Shelley and the more passionate phases of Browning's art. With Spenser, we think of Keats and William Morris.

His genius is epic, not lyric; he is a story-teller, not a singer. He has something of Homer's ancient simplicity, though not the poignancy. But the similes are primal and direct.

A wounded hero falls

> ". . . as an aged tree,
> High growing on the top of rocky clift."

His is a rich ornate imagination; yet it rarely becomes turbid and oppressive. If it lacks Marlowe's thrill, it certainly also lacks his violence. It is a thing of prismatic colouring, refracting the white light of common day in delicate rainbow hues. The symbolism behind his faërie music need not trouble us; and we may enjoy the adventures of his Knight of the Cross defending his belovéd Una, almost without realising that it is the battle between truth and falsehood with which he is concerned.

And yet the mingling of Puritanism and sensuous pleasure is one of the chief charms, just as it was that of a great successor —Milton.

The world of Chivalry supplies him with his poetic imagery. He has drunk of that magical stream of Romance that inspired the old Arthurian cycle. In his company we hear "the horns of Elfland faintly blowing." Through the witchery of his genius the rude legends of the past are bereft of their roughness and barbarity, and shine like polished gems.

So far the poetry passed under notice has been of the stately and sentimental kind. To find a livelier mood we must turn to a school of poetry which sprang up about the time of Spenser —the lyric school, and gave expression to the more sensitive moods of the Elizabethan.

The lyric was already a literary force both in Italy and France; but until 1580 it did not impress itself upon English imagination. What brought about the sudden flowering of the lyric? To some extent the persistent study of foreign poetry, but chiefly the growing popularity of music.

Such brilliant musicians as Byrd, Tallis, and Dowland needed articulate expression for their sweet lute melodies. The gift of song no doubt was dormant in many an Elizabethan verse-writer. It needed some outside stimulus to call it forth, and assuredly at no time in our history has there been so rich a company of singers; some already famous in other directions as dramatists or novelists, many quite unknown save for their "short swallow flights of song."

William Byrd is the earliest of these singers, but his verse is characterized by its quaint moralising rather than by any flight of fancy. Lighter in texture are the Songs of John Dowland, famed for his "heavenly touch upon the lute." In the last years of the sixteenth century he published two volumes of "Songs and Airs." Take this charming snatch from the first volume (1597)—

"Dear, if you change, I'll never choose again;
Sweet, if you shrink, I'll never think of love;
Fair, if you fail, I'll judge all beauty vain;
Wise, if too weak, more wits I'll never prove.
Dear, sweet, fair, wise! Change, shrink, nor be not weak;
And, on my faith, my faith shall never break."

Campion distinguished himself in three capacities, putting aside his fame as a musician. He wrote masques, among the best of their kind; displayed his nimble wit and scholarship in Latin verse; and discussed in prose form the values of music and poetry.

Campion's songs are light as thistledown, and float away in the air.

Following these came John Daniel, Robert Jones, Thomas Morley, and in the early years of the seventeenth century a crowd of names, about whom in many cases little is known save for the gay and tender lyrics ascribed to them. Before leaving them we must not overlook the splendid profusion of lyrical wealth to be found in the Elizabethan dramas and masques, from the boisterous humour of *Ralph Roister Doister*, through the work of Lyly, Greene, Lodge, and Nash, the mighty structure of Shakespeare, down to Heywood, Fletcher, and Sir William Davenant. In the post-Shakespearean drama, Beaumont and Fletcher—the best all-round dramatists—are likewise the freshest and most melodious singers; Fletcher's contributions being especially musical.

During the earlier years of the seventeenth century, the poetry of the time shows the influence of two distinct schools. Just as the dramatists of the day follow the leadership of Shakespeare or Ben Jonson, so do the poets model themselves upon Spenser or Donne. The Spenserian school are allegorical and descriptive; the school of Donne meditative and lyrical.

The Spenserian School.—The most important names here are those of the brothers Giles and Phineas Fletcher (cousins of John Fletcher, the dramatist), Drummond of Hawthornden, William Browne, and George Wither. Giles Fletcher's long poem, *Christ's Victory and Triumph* (1610), is obviously inspired by the *Faërie Queene*, and has something of its sweetness and richness. Its special significance lies in the fact that it bridges the narrative romance of Spenser and the religious epic of Milton, suggesting at once the manner of the elder Elizabethan poet and the matter of the last of the great Renascence writers. The pastoral and allegorical note of Spenser is discernible also in Phineas Fletcher's *Purple Island;* and there is descriptive vigour and beauty in the *Pastorals* (1613) of the Devonshire poet, William Browne; George Wither, the most prolific of this little group, is also the most unequal, but at his best can reproduce effectively the lingering sweetness of Spenser. His well-known "Shall I wasting in despair?" is said to have been written while he was imprisoned in the Marshalsea.

The School of Donne.—There were before Donne writers like Davies and Fulke Greville (Lord Brooke), whose temperaments inclined them to philosophical subjects. But Donne is the great personality to develop and emphasize the reflective vein.

John Donne, with his passionate nature and restless vitality, like many of the literary men of his age, was a man of action as well as a man of letters. Erratic and pleasure-loving in his youth, he passed, like St. Francis d'Assisi, from one extreme to another in the course of his life, and in his later years as Dean of St. Paul's proved a preacher of great emotional power, "always preaching to himself," as his biographer Izaak Walton said, "like an angel from a cloud, but in none."

The bulk of his poetry was written in earlier years, and despite the extravagance and obscurity of much of his work, is finely musical, while its note of wistful meditation inspired many who excelled their master in sweetness and clarity.

Among those who came under his influence may be mentioned the accomplished Lord Herbert of Cherbury, the first to use the metre of *In Memoriam*; Robert Herrick, most delightful of hedonistic clerics; Suckling, fertile in dainty conceits; unhappy Lovelace, famous for his "Loved I not Honour more"; that ardent mystic, Richard Crashaw; brilliant Carew; Henry Vaughan and George Herbert, men of more delicate clay, in whose verse the puritanical quaintness of Donne's poetry is more observable.

Last in this pleasant company of singers is Edmund Waller, admirable as a stylist, but lacking the warmth and unstudied grace of his predecessors, save in one or two short pieces, especially the charming song, "Go, lovely rose."

Drayton.—One poet hard to classify, because of the great variety of his work, is Michael Drayton. Indeed it is for his variety, not for any special excellence, that he is notable. And he had undoubted versatility, giving us a topographical poem, *The Polyolbion*, of genuine interest; some accomplished lyrics, an admirable war song, *The Ballad of Agincourt*, and an ingenious fantasy, *Nymphadia*.

John Milton.—In his literary parentage he owes somewhat to both Donne and Spenser, and in a slight degree to Ben Jonson. But his debts were slight as compared with the rich legacy he gave to English poetry; and it has been justly said that he represented the fourth great influence in English prosody. Chaucer had transformed Middle English into a robust force; and Spenser and Shakespeare gave—the one to narrative, the other to dramatic poetry—a sweetness and variety impossible to overrate. Then there came a period largely of imitation and elaboration, rather than of any great originality. English poetry between the time of Shakespeare and Milton has many gifts and graces, but the quality of greatness is denied it, and it was left for Milton to restore this quality to our poetry. He is the last word in the English Renascence. Gradually but surely its splendour had been fading away, but in Milton it flames up into a glorious sunset, and, like the sunset, touched by a grave and pensive beauty peculiarly its own.

The serious and meditative spirit infused by Puritanism into the poetry of the time turned Milton's thoughts from such subjects as the Arthurian Legend (once considered by him), and his epic genius found perfect expression in the biblical story of the Fall of Man. Nothing is more characteristic of the poet than the arduous mental development he deliberately set before himself in order to grapple with his task. The earlier years of his life were spent in hard study and preparation; then for a while he plunged into fierce political controversy in the cause of civil and religious liberty: finally, in the last years of his life he gave us, as the fruit of his mature genius, *Paradise Lost*, *Paradise Regained*, and *Samson Agonistes.*

Sense of Beauty.—Possessing a sense of beauty, as keen though less unrestrained than that possessed by the Elizabethans, Milton's devotion to form and coherence separate him from the great Romantics, and give to the beauty of his verse a delicacy and gravity all their own. Like Jonson he favoured the classical conventions rather than the happy-go-lucky methods of Romanticism; but unlike Jonson he never allowed his scholarship to chill his creative imagination. Nowhere is this quality of beauty better displayed than in the early poems, in *Allegro, Penseroso*, *Comus*, and *Lycidas.* They have all the freshness and charm of youth, and exhibit the lighter and more fanciful side of Milton's genius.

As an illustration, take the image in his address to Melancholy:

"Come, pensive nun, devout and pure."

A Stateliness of Manner.—And with this sense of beauty is combined a stateliness of manner which gives a high dignity to Milton's poetry, that has never been surpassed, and rarely equalled in our literature.

The dramatic possibilities of blank verse had been developed to a wonderful degree by Marlowe and Shakespeare, but in their successors it had to some extent deteriorated. Jonson's classical severity was not combined with any considerable beauty or distinction; and the increasing looseness of texture in the plays favoured a slovenly tendency in the blank verse of the day. In the lighter form of verse, and in the lyric, there was no such falling off; but the more ambitious and elaborate forms of non-dramatic poetry stood in need of some influence at once chastening and inspiring. In his great epic, Milton is extraordinarily fertile in the methods he adopts to avoid monotony. He strengthens blank verse without cramping it; he gives it grace without making it vapid, and rounds off with finished care the single line without ever sacrificing the organic unity of the entire poem. He is like a great organist who, while never losing sight of the ancient melody, adorns it with every conceivable variation which serves to show up, in place of obscuring, the freshness and sweetness of the simple theme.

The decadence of the drama was in itself a sufficient testimony to the disintegrating forces of the day. Austerity was needed by any man of letters who would raise our literature again to a noble level. And none used this quality with more unflinching purpose than Milton. No doubt it made him unpopular. Perhaps no great poet was ever accounted so little by his own generation as Milton. But his greatness was not for long undiscovered.

The modern reader may regard with but languid interest the celestial pageant that Milton unrolls before him in his lengthy epics, but the merits of *Paradise Lost* and *Paradise Regained* do not depend upon the reader's taste in theology, but upon the stark grandeur of many descriptive passages, and the passionate love of Nature which glows throughout the poet's work. It meets us first in the fresh sweetness of *L'Allegro* and *Il Penseroso:*

"Russet leaves and fallows grey,
Where the nibbling flocks do stray;
Mountain on whose barren breast
The labouring clouds do often rest;
Meadows trim with daisies pied,
Shallow brooks and rivers wide"

gains strength and dignity in *Lycidas:*

"While the still morn went out with sandals grey,"

and thrills us with sublime splendour in *Paradise Lost* and *Samson Agonistes:*

". . . airs, vernal airs
Breathing the smell of field and grove, attune

The trembling leaves while Universal Pan,
Knit with the Graces and the Hours in dance,
Led on the Eternal Spring."

3. The Novel

The eager inquisitive spirit that flamed up at the Renascence could not exhaust itself entirely in the expansion of our poetry, or even in the creation of the romantic drama; for in achieving this it realised also the compelling interest of everyday actualities.

Had it not been for Italy the Novel might have tarried for another hundred years. Rhetoric and song were indigenous to the race; Spenser, Marlowe, Shakespeare would have found articulate speech, Italy or no Italy. But it may reasonably be doubted whether we should have had the Elizabethan novelist.

Why was the influence of Italy so suddenly and imperatively felt?

Largely because of the newly awakened rage of the day for foreign travel, which helped to spread Italian fashions both of dress and literature.

And Italy was the home of the Novel. It was here Boccaccio in 1350 first attempted those prose tales of amorous adventure, *The Decameron*—"Novella Storia." The term originally meant a *fresh* story, but soon novel was applied to *any* story in *prose* as distinct from a story in verse, which retained its old appellation of Romance.

Travel stimulated also the translation of Italian literature. So that those who could not afford to travel could at least learn something of this literary El Dorado through translations.

The mediæval Romance dealt with a legendary past. The Novel dealt with the realities of everyday life. In this lay its compelling attraction.

There was no more popular book than William Painter's collection of Italian Stories. He was the Clerk of the Ordnance in the Tower, and his translation not merely inspired the Romantic Drama but interested English readers in Italian fiction specifically, and the art form of the Novel generally.

The Elizabethan prose writers who distinguished themselves in prose fiction were John Lyly, Robert Greene, Thomas Lodge, Sir Philip Sidney, and Thomas Nash.

John Lyly is the pioneer of the English Novel, the first stylist in prose, and the most popular writer of his age. A young Kentish man, with slender financial resources and very few friends, he had the good fortune to attract the attention of Lord Burleigh, who became his patron.

In 1579 Lyly published the first part of his famous fiction, *Euphues, the Anatomy of Wit.*

Euphues was a good-looking, nimble-minded Athenian youth who goes first to Naples, then to England to study men and governments. His volubility is remarkable, and he uses his friend Philautus as a kind of conversational Aunt Sally against whom to hurl his sententious wisdom. Once indeed during the voyage to England Philautus does rebel: "In faith, Euphues, thou hast told a long tale, the beginning I have forgotten, the middle I understand not, and the end hangeth not together . . . in the meantime it were best for me to take a nap, for I cannot brook these seas, which provoke my stomach sore."

The story itself is slight, with a mild love interest, the chief value of the book lying in its picture of English customs and its peculiarities of style.

The style is marked by the constant use of antithesis and alliteration, which at times becomes mannered to a wearisome extent, but often gives agreeable force and pungency to the matter:

> ". . . Where salt doth grow nothing else can breed.
> Where friendship is built no offence can harbour."

Often, too, there is humour:

> "It is a blind goose that cometh to the fox's sermon."
> "Thou must halt cunningly to beguile a cripple."

And yet Lyly's prose is prose which has not yet shaken off the ornaments of verse. It is the prose of an age that could find its speech far more readily in song and sonnet.

Robert Greene, who succeeded Lyly, if less brilliant, attains a greater simplicity in his later writings.

He was a happy-go-lucky Bohemian, who had no patron, and lived on his wits. His first novel is poor and imitative, but in *Pandosto* (1588), from which Shakespeare took his *Winter's Tale*, he showed real originality. The most considerable factor made by Greene to the development of the novel is to be found in his pamphlets rather than in his conventional fiction, for here he writes from personal knowledge of the "underworld" of his day. Especially vivid is his *Life and Death of Ned Browne*, a notorious cut-purse, wherein he anticipates the "low life" scenes of Defoe and Smollett.

Another writer of fiction to be noted is Thomas Lodge, the studious friend of Greene. He travelled much in the earlier years of his life, and while journeying he wrote several romances —one entitled *Rosalynde* (1590), which inspired Shakespeare's *As You Like It.*

The fourth important name in the fiction of the time is *Thomas Nash.* "Ingenuous, ingenious, fluent, facetious Thomas Nash," as his friend Lodge called him. The emphatic quality was the facetiousness. There was a strain of humour in Lyly, and fitful outbursts of gaiety in Greene, but both Lodge and Sidney showed rather a contemplative wit than humour or mirthfulness. It is otherwise with Nash; he has a rich fund of humour that partakes somewhat of Rabelais' uproarious quality.

Nash, like Greene, took the rogue in hand and painted with skill and fidelity the needy adventurer of the time: *The Unfortunate Traveller, or The Life of Jack Wilton* (1594), but unlike his contemporary he did so with a smile on his lips. He found the English novel suffering from too much sentiment, and promptly freshened it with his light-hearted humour.

He died at the age of thirty-three, having shortened his days, says his friend Dekker, "by keeping company with pickled herrings."

Eschewing the literary affectations and manners of his day, he did his best to cultivate an individual style, vigorous, easy and vital, one well suited to his subject-matter. He is the precursor of Fielding; Lyly the progenitor of Richardson.

Sidney's Arcadia.—Of Sidney's work as a poet mention has been made. His *Arcadia* remains to be noticed, for it marks a well-defined stage in the history of the novel.

Preceding writers had been more or less disciples of Lyly and imitators of Euphuism. Sidney invented a new style. And for a while Arcadianism displaced Euphuism. This book, written in 1580, appeared after Sidney's death. It was written primarily to please his sister, the Countess of Pembroke. In essence it is a romance with a pastoral flavouring. There is more characterisation and more movement, though less humour, than we find in Lyly; more passion than in Greene, if less actuality: and a finer vein of poetry than in Lodge, though more unequal in interest. The style, despite artificialities, rises at times to a level of high beauty. With Lyly's *Euphues* it may take its place as one of the dominant influences of the time.

French influences more considerably affect Sidney than his predecessors. Perhaps he is, of all of them, the least touched by the magic of Italy, though he was a great admirer of Spanish literature.

Dekker, whose dramatic work has already been noticed, also essayed fiction. But although he had some measure of Nash's gaiety and shrewdness of observation in the "Picaresque" stories which he essayed, it is as a dramatist and writer of prose, other than fiction, that he is most entitled to remembrance. With the close of the Elizabethan period the first period of the English novel came to an end. During the next century, French romance of the extravagant and artificial order came into fashion for the class who cared about fiction. But, as we shall see, if the seventeenth century produced no great novelist, it produced many writers who contributed indirectly to the amazing development of the Novel which took place in the eighteenth century.

4. Prose other than Fiction

In the prose of the age Roger Ascham, that sturdy Puritan scholar, provides a suitable starting-point.

He effectually broke away from the elder traditions that gave Latin preference to English, and favoured good, direct English prose. His distaste for romance and the influence of modern Italy kept his prose somewhat cramped and colourless. But there are two treatises extant of his, one on *Shooting*, the other on *School-mastering*, which, if lacking in flexibility of style, none the less exhibit him as a writer of direct, orderly English.

Ascham gave English prose clarity; Lyly imported colour and animation into it; and Sidney, both in his *Arcadia* and in his admirable *Apologie for Poetrie* (1581), gave it sweetness.

Here is an extract from the description of the Vale of Arcadia:

"... Here a shepherd's boy piping as though he should never be old; there a young shepherdess knitting, and withal singing, and it seemed that her voice comforted her hands to work, and her hands kept time to her voice music."

Richard Hooker, the famous preacher and controversialist, added to these qualities that of dignity. Self-restrained in his dialectic, he is equally self-restrained in his style. Less fantastic than Lyly, less exuberant than Sidney, there is a power and a balance about his writing that none of his predecessors could achieve.

The most considerable name at the close of the Elizabethan age is that of Francis Bacon. His cool, judicious temperament failed to attract the Queen, and this enabled his uncle Burleigh, and cousin Robert Cecil, to keep him from opportunities of rising; but on her death he rapidly made his way, for James took considerable interest in him, and it was during the later part of his life that the bulk of his literary work was done. Although he had no great respect for the English language, holding that "these modern languages will at one time play the bankrupt with books," yet no man individually did more to give strength and simplicity to our tongue than he. So far, the great defect in English prose was its prolixity and diffuseness. Bacon put an end to this, and his Essays are, even to this day, a model of terse, easy English. With his philosophical and scientific treatises, such as the *Novum Organum*, we need not concern ourselves here. From our point of view the chief writings to notice are the *Essays*, the *Advancement of Learning*, the *History of Henry VII*, and the *New Atlantis*.

The keynote of the *New Atlantis* is the pursuit of knowledge, which in Bacon's view is a religious duty. The College of Research, which he pictures in his fragmentary sketch, anticipates the Royal Society, which sprang into being later, and served as a model (admitted by Diderot) for the French Encyclopædia of the eighteenth century. Many of the scientific hints thrown out by Bacon as Utopian possibilities have now become everyday realities. Certainly we may claim to have "some Degrees of Flying in the Ayre . . . ships and Boates for going under water." Modern medical science is familiar with "Chambers of Health where we qualify the Aire . . . for the cure of divers Diseases." These are but a few illustrations of the way in which Bacon foreshadowed the trend of scientific research.

The style of the book is clear and direct. Comparing it as a Utopian picture with that of More, a few points of interest detach themselves.

(1) More emphasizes the social; Bacon the intellectual well-being of the community.

(2) The chief note in More's *Utopia* is simplicity of life, whereas the chief feature of the citizens of *Atlantis* is orderliness of life.

(3) More is puritan in his ideas of dress; Bacon favours a certain external splendour.

(4) The tone of More's mind is democratic; of Bacon's aristocratic.

Bacon's fragment, equally with More's more considerable work, has inspired future generations no less by its fertile suggestions than by its simple charm of narrative.

Excellent in another way is the sketch of *Henry VII*. A

lucid, vigorous piece of historical narrative, with touches of vivid characterisation.

Turning to the *Essays*, we note the intimate ease of the style. If Montaigne is the first great Essayist, Bacon is certainly the first great English Essayist. He saw clearly that the art of the Essay is in reality the art of Conversation; that the main thing was to get into familiar touch with the reader, and this could only be done by avoiding misty rhetoric and formal mannerisms, and stating the subject simply, clearly, and tersely. No other Essayist, with the exception of Emerson, has shown so condensed and aphoristic a style. And like Emerson, he throws off a succession of pithy epigrammatic sayings. "No man," said Ben Jonson, "ever spake more neatly, more precisely, more weightily, or suffered less emptiness, less idleness in what he uttered . . ."

Along with Bacon may be mentioned Jonson, whose *Discoveries* are written in a style that for terseness and lucidity is little inferior to Bacon's.

Influence of the Bible.—*The Authorised Version of the Bible*, which appeared early in the seventeenth century, was to mould and colour the literature of the succeeding centuries. The translators took the fullest advantage of the literary beauty of their matter, assisted by the excellent rough material provided for them by earlier English versions.

Indirectly, of course, since Saxon times, Hebrew song had glorified English prose; and in Cædmon's *Hymn*, where English literature found its earliest expression, we have the rhythm and parallelism peculiar to Hebrew poetry. Moreover, Hebraic idioms occur continually in the prose of Aelfred and Aelfric, Wyclif and Langland.

But the effect of the Authorised Version was to intensify enormously the influence of the Bible on the prose of the time.

The greatness of English prose dates from the translation of the Bible, and although English poetry is far less dependent for its excellence upon Hebrew inspiration, even here a weight, dignity, and richness were added to it.

During the Caroline times the influence of the Authorised Version may clearly be traced in the prose of the time. It gives dignity to such historians as Clarendon and Fuller, a sober eloquence to the devotional outpourings of Jeremy Taylor, and an ease and grace to the quaint fancies of Sir Thomas Browne's *Religio Medici* (1642) and *Urn Burial* (1658), and the discursive wit of the *Anatomy of Melancholy* (1621), by Robert Burton.

Milton's prose, in his earlier days, has more of the rough vigour and directness of Elizabethan polemics than the strength and beauty of its greater prose. But two of his pamphlets rise to a higher level: *The Areopagitica, or Speech for the Liberty of Unlicensed Printing* (1644), and the tract on *Education* (1644).

If Milton is the last word in the poetry of the English Renascence, Bunyan is the last word in prose. In both of them Puritanism finds eloquent speech. We can imagine neither of them well without the Authorised Version—least of all Bunyan. Milton's style also is steeped in classicism; but Bunyan, simple and unlettered, derives directly from the Bible. There is an epic quality about *The Pilgrim's Progress* (1677) which has the rare merit of touching the imagination of both the scholar and the uncultured man. Had he been born a hundred years earlier, we might have had another and finer Nash. Undoubtedly he had the instinct of the novelist, for his characterisation is clear and strong, his dialogue alive, and his descriptive power vigorous and picturesque. Then there is such unpremeditated art and sincerity in the writing. Sincerity and vigour inform also *The Holy War* (1684) and *Grace Abounding* (1666), but there is less attempt at literary form here. Mention must be made of that remarkable fiction, *The Life and Death of Mr. Badman* (1680), which, despite its comparative brevity, challenges equality with *The Pilgrim's Progress.* The English Novel in the eighteenth century owed a heavy debt to John Bunyan.

III

THE AGE OF SATIRE (*c.* 1660–1740)

(*From Butler to Pope*)

Introduction.—About the middle of the seventeenth century a change began to come over the spirit of English literature. This change is due to no mere fluctuation of literary fashion, but is deeply rooted in the life of the time. The age of the Renascence was an age of spiritual and material expansion. Englishmen realised for the first time their solidarity as a nation; and released suddenly from continental struggles, especially from the dread of Spanish supremacy, they found an outlet for their excited emotions in drama and song. Loyalty to Elizabeth became a flaming passion; pride and delight in their country's past a religious faith. This spirit is reflected in the *Faërie Queene*, and in the historical plays of Marlowe and Shakespeare.

But the emotional fervour was too high pitched to last. Already in the early years of the seventeenth century its splendid exuberance had degenerated into extravagance and violence. The lofty idealism that had steadied the venturesome bark of Elizabethan poesy was growing attenuated, and the great minds in the closing years of the age, like Bacon and Milton, reflect in their writings the dawn of fresh interests. The purification of civic and political life emerges more and more into the forefront. Shakespeare and Ben Jonson stand aloof from the political problems of the hour. Bacon and Milton are active politicians no less than great writers. But until the Restoration, the full significance of this change is not realised. It meets us first of all in the later poems of Abraham Cowley, and in the polished verse of Edmund Waller and Sir John Denham; it frankly and unmistakably proclaims itself a new note in our literature with the coming of Dryden.

What are the Characteristics of this Change?—*The Dominance of the Critical Spirit in place of the Imaginative Spirit.* Such a change is inevitable when literature is made the vehicle of attacking the political life of the day. The creative imagination moves on the plane of primal human qualities: it is concerned with the interpretation of human nature, and although passing movements may give a local habitation and a name to some of its dioramic pictures, the main object is not to criticise the life of the day but to interpret it.

The new spirit, however, is above all critical and analytic: not creative and synthetic; it brings the intellect rather than the poetic imagination into play. And the merits of the new school are to be found in its intellectual force and actuality; just as its demerits lie in its lack of deep imagination, and tendency to deal with manners and superficialities, rather than with elemental things and the larger issues of life.

Reasons for the Change.—This change is due partly to the conditions of English political and social life, partly to the influence of France, which early in the seventeenth century threw off the flowery traditions of the Italian Renascence, and declared itself in favour of literary sobriety and restraint. The French poet Malherbe, early in the seventeenth century, had pioneered the movement, and in 1673 Boileau counselled his countrymen to write with "good sense" and avoid Italian rhapsody.

So it will be seen that the new age follows in the wake of Jonson, not of Shakespeare. Such a change was better adapted for a kind of literature which aimed especially at clearness, conciseness, and concentrated force. The less attractive aspect of this ideal is seen in the verse of the day; the finer and more valuable aspects in its prose.

The object of the leading writers of the time was to avoid extravagance and emotionalism. This in many cases they did so successfully as to suppress altogether the emotional and basic qualities of great poetry, though their method found congenial expression in the satire.

Poetry, starved of emotional sustenance, had to fall back on epigram, but the "good sense" ideal was an admirable one for prose. For if we examine the aims of the prose writers of the day, we shall find that their supreme object is to be simple in style and natural in manner.

"The Royal Society," declared the Bishop of Rochester, "have exacted from all their members a close, marked, natural way of speaking; positive expressions, clear sense, a native easiness, bringing all things as near the mathematical plainness as they can; and preferring the language of artisans, countrymen and merchants before that of wits and scholars."

This is unequivocal enough, and as we shall see, when we consider the prose of the age, the ideal here enunciated was triumphantly put into practice. In the drama alone, which had come to be a courtiers' game, is artificiality of prose upheld. There, for the sake of amusement, lucidity and directness are made subsidiary to the brilliance of wit and stylic graces.

1. Poetry

One result of the characteristic touched upon above is that the poetry of this new age is marked by the substitution of humour for passion.

Humour played a subsidiary part in Renascence literature; now it is the prime factor, and the form in which it is expressed is called the *satire.*

The note of satire is discernible in some of the Caroline singers, but the two names of greatest importance are the puritan, Andrew Marvel, and anti-puritan, Samuel Butler. Butler can be effective enough at times, as in the picture of Sir Hudibras' Presbyterian followers, who

> "Call fire and sword and desolation,
> A godly thorough Reformation;
> Compound for sins they are inclined to,
> By damning those they have no mind to."

The first English verse satire had been Gascoigne's *Steele Glas* (1576), but it stands by itself, and there was no other satirical verse until the time of Donne.

JOHN DRYDEN is the first exponent of the movement. With great intellectual power and a remarkable aptitude for expressing himself clearly and succinctly in vigorous verse, he gave us his great poem, *Absalom and Achitophel* (1681), after a long apprenticeship of playwriting. This satire, political in trend, attacked the politicians of the day—Shaftesbury was Achitophel, Monmouth was Absalom—with a mordant wit that compelled attention. A later poetical work was his *Fables, Ancient and Modern* (1700), which show an easy mastery of verse and an acumen unsurpassed by any of his contemporaries.

The distinctive qualities of Dryden as a poet are ease, variety of method, and vigour.

In the heroic couplet, the decasyllabic quatrain, and in blank verse he showed equal mastery. But it was in the heroic couplet that he achieved his strongest effects. It lacks the chiselled nicety of form and epigrammatic brilliance brought to it by his successor, Pope; but has a richer and more vital body about it; and as a master of prosody, Dryden ranks with Milton and Shakespeare.

Dryden, like Jonson, was the literary dictator of his age; presiding at Wills' Coffee House in undisputed supremacy among the wits of his time.

His successor, ALEXANDER POPE, was a man of more feminine temperament, though equally imbued with the same critical spirit. But whereas in Dryden's case we get broad massive effects, as a rule, in Pope we have delicate filigree work. Unlike Dryden—unlike most other poets indeed, Pope seems to have served no apprenticeship to literature. His first poem, *The Essay in Criticism* (1711), is as careful in phrasing, as equally polished, and as admirable in craftsmanship as the mature *Essay on Man* (1732–34.)

As a satirist, his range is less wide than Dryden's, and he cannot achieve the sinewy ease of "glorious John." But along his own lines, admittedly restricted, his wit is even keener, and for sheer lightness of touch and mordant delicacy his "boudoir" satire. *The Rape of the Lock* (1712) is perfect. The artificial tone of the age, the frivolous aspect of femininity is nowhere more exquisitely pictured than in this poem. It is the epic of triflings; a page torn from the petty, pleasure-seeking life of a fashionable beauty; the *mise-en-scène* the toilet chamber and the card table. In short, the veritable apotheosis in literary guise of scent, patches, and powder.

Pope's success as a writer naturally made for him a number of enemies, many of whom, obscure and penniless men, it would have been best to treat with good-natured silence. They were too feeble to injure Pope's reputation, and to attack them scurrilously, as he did in the *Dunciad* (1728), showed an unpleasing smallness of nature. As the rough but essentially good-natured Johnson said, "Whom did it concern to know that one scribbler or another was a Dunce!"

The work of Pope is rich in aphorisms and apothegms. There is no poet, Shakespeare excepted, whose sayings have so freely enriched our language. And it is not through any greatness of imagination or freshness of insight, but by virtue of a singular power, to transform an ordinary idea, a commonplace morality, into a neat and pungent phrase.

For instance:

> "Worth makes the man, and want of it the fellow,
> The rest is all but leather or prunella."
> (*Essay on Man.*)

> "A little learning is a dangerous thing—
> Drink deep, or taste not the Pierian spring."
> (*Essay on Criticism.*)

During the later period of Pope's life a reaction started in English poetry, which is best considered when dealing with the Romantic movement of the nineteenth century; but during the greater part of Pope's life his lesser contemporaries follow the general lines initiated by Dryden. Addison's verse is marked by culture and grace, whilst a blither note is struck by John Gay in his *Shepherd's Week*. Gay, most companionable of *bon viveurs*, has given us some agreeable sketches of London manners and fashions, and his light-hearted gift of song finds expression in *Black-Eyed Susan* and *The Beggar's Opera*. Gay belonged to Pope's circle; another associate is "Matt" Prior, a gay trifler, who had the gift of expressing his easy cynicism in excellent verse. He more nearly approaches Pope than any other contemporary in the technical excellence of his work and in epigrammatic power.

2. The Drama

William Congreve, one of the most brilliant dramatists of the age, told Voltaire on one occasion that he wished to be regarded not as a literary man, but as a gentleman.

This pious opinion is indicative of the tone of the time. The drama was no longer, as it was in Elizabethan days, an expression of the national life; but a picture of "polite society." In Shakespeare's day it had been a national recreation, now it was merely a fashionable pastime.

The influence of France is more pronounced in the drama than in either the poetry or prose. French Romances were ransacked for plots, and the methods and situations of Corneille, Racine, and especially Molière, may be traced in much of the dramatic literature of the time. As might be expected, the age excelled in comedy rather than in tragedy; the most remarkable of the tragedies being by THOMAS OTWAY, *The Orphan* (1680), and *Venice Preserved* (1682). These are rich in emotional situations, but are not in any way comparable with the tragedies of the Elizabethans.

Dryden, whose figure dominates here, as in the realm of verse and of prose, experimented in both comedy and tragedy. His tragedies, the *Indian Queen* (1664) and the *Indian Emperor* (published 1667), popularised for fourteen years the rhymed couplet in drama. This was an innovation from the French, and for a while put out of favour the old blank verse. In 1678, however, he returned to blank verse in his best tragedy, *All for Love*. In addition to these plays he is responsible for some excellent comedies; for instance *The Spanish Friar* (1681) and *Amphitryon*.

The comedy, however, developed further in the hands of Sir George Etheredge, Mrs. Behn, and Shadwell; and was brought to its highest pitch by Wycherley, Congreve, Vanbrugh, and Farquhar.

WYCHERLEY, for all his skill in intrigue, as illustrated in *Love in a Wood* (1672) and *The Country Wife* (1675), is inferior both in invention and wit to Congreve. Of Congreve's Plays, the best are *The Double Dealer* (1693) and *The Way of the World* (1700); excellent alike in their acting qualities and their literary power. Superior in wit and more agreeable in quality are *The Relapse* (1697) and *The Confederacy* (1705) of VANBRUGH, an architect of Flemish descent; and *The Recruiting Officer* (1706) and *Beaux Stratagem* (1707) of FARQUHAR, the first of the many brilliant Irishmen who have enriched our stage.

Satiric comedy was followed during Queen Anne's time by a period of sentimental comedy, pioneered by Steele. Another type of comedy was started in Gay's *Beggar's Opera* (1727), and during the later years of the eighteenth century sentiment and satire blended in the fresher and sweeter work of GOLDSMITH'S *Good-Natured Man* (1768) and *She Stoops to Conquer* (1773), while the witty métier of Congreve found a revivalist in Sheridan, who had much of Congreve's inventive power and Vanbrugh's polish, with none of their coarseness. With SHERIDAN the age of the elder comedy of manners practically closes. His is the last great name in the drama of the eighteenth century.

3. PROSE

Whenever intellectual rather than sheerly imaginative qualities dominate the literature of a period, the prose invariably proves of more commanding importance than the poetry. The logical faculty and the gift of critical insight find freer and more suitable expression in language unfettered by rhyme or metre. Such is the case here. The poetry is interesting of its kind, but its kind is extremely limited; the drama, halfway-house between prose and verse, excels in comedy spirit, but on the more serious side cannot compare in any way with the rich intensity of Elizabethan tragedy: that is to say, it excels where intellect, not high imagination, is called for.

The prose, however, while in certain directions it feels necessarily the lowering of the poetic temperature, is on the whole on a higher and firmer plane than it has ever been before. Elizabethan prose vacillated between the ultra-ornate and the ultra-bald; occasionally in a Hooker or Bacon it achieved an austere grace or a stately brevity, but its tendency is in the direction of verbosity and elaborate ornamentation, and this somewhat arbitrarily conditions its effectiveness. So while its merits and charm are often undeniable, it lacks that directness, simplicity, and ease which are the distinguishing marks of prose in an age of Dryden and Pope.

Traces of this new school may be found in the later prose of Cowley, the sober, historical method of Clarendon in his *History of the Great Rebellion* (1707), and the *Leviathan* (1651) of Hobbes, which discovered the new divine right of the people, as opposed to the old theory of the divine right of kings. Dryden, however, is the first great exponent and pioneer. His interest in dramatic literature led him to write, about 1685, his well-known *Essay on Dramatic Poesy*, which, besides containing fine and discriminating criticism of the English drama, is an admirable example of plain, direct, and vital prose; this, without becoming vulgar or slipshod, achieves an easy and intimate note especially telling, and can on occasion reach dignity and eloquence without resource to windy rhetoric.

In the sermons of John Tillotson, this plain sobriety of

language receives further illustration. One has only to compare the matter-of-fact style of Tillotson, for instance his St. Paul's sermon on the *Wisdom of being Religious*, with the ornate brilliance of Jeremy Taylor to appreciate the effect of the new spirit.

Two names of greater literary importance are those of Sir William Temple and the Marquis of Halifax (George Savile). Their work marks the beginnings of the modern Essay. Temple, husband of that most delightful letter-writer, Dorothy Osborne, best displays his literary gifts in his *Miscellanies*. These essays on various subjects—Health, Gout, Gardening, Poetry—are written in clear, agreeable, unaffected style, rising at times to a rhythmic beauty, as in the *Essay on Poetry*. They certainly show that the ease and intimacy of the New School need not be divorced from dignity and beauty. Halifax was a political force as well as a man of letters; achieved fame with his pamphlet, *The Character of a Trimmer*, which indicates accurately his own political attitude; became famous as a parliamentary speaker; and in a volume of *Miscellanies* (*c.* 1688), which contained essays on various subjects and a few notable pamphlets, showed grace, lucidity, and terseness. He writes more like the man of the world than Temple, and his aphorisms have a pleasant satirical flavour, as that on *An Empty Woman:* "Such an one is seldom serious but with her tailor;" or this, "You may love your children without living in the nursery."

Of considerable influence upon the development of English prose is the work of the famous diarist Pepys—inquisitive, childish, vain, delightful Pepys. Considerable, for it encouraged a more intimate and homely style. Of less significance is the *Diary* of his elder and more staid contemporary Evelyn, and the quaintly colloquial *Lives* of Roger North.

If the ease and simplicity of the new school of writers may be seen in Dryden and Pepys, its clarity in Temple, its worldly common sense in Halifax, its matter-of-factness is nowhere better shown than in the work of the philosopher John Locke. Just as the trend of his work signifies the apotheosis of practical common sense, so does his style reflect the spirit of common sense. It is clear, thoughtful, to the point, devoid of all flowers of speech, never aspiring to eloquence, eschewing humour, pathos, and the graces dear to the essayist; yet preserved from dullness and triteness by the dignity of his subject and by the intellectual force of the writer.

Joseph Addison and Sir Richard Steele.—"Whoever wishes," says Dr. Johnson, "to attain an English style, familiar but not coarse, and elegant but not ostentatious, must give his days and nights to the volumes of Addison." Posterity has endorsed the essential justice of Johnson's tribute. The more urbane aspects of eighteenth-century prose are nowhere better exhibited than in the prose of Addison. Steele's writing shows greater warmth and vigour, but for delicate charm Addison excels.

In 1709 Steele started *The Tatler*, which inaugurated a fresh epoch in the development of prose.

We are approaching now the existence in London of a definite literary class. The man of letters in the ages preceding depended for his livelihood upon a patron.

Patronage still exists, and Pope made his fortune by what has been called "a kind of joint-stock patronage," where the aristocratic patron found it convenient to induce his friends to subscribe towards the maintenance of the poet. But the older system was dying out.

At first the poet or the pamphleteer attaches himself to some influential Minister, using his pen on behalf of this gentleman's cause. Afterwards, when the Minister found he could get his work done more cheaply than by hiring men of taste, the literary man gets thrown upon the suffrages of a public then rising into existence.

The coffee-house, and later the clubs, were centres around which radiated the thoughtful and intelligent: politicians, lawyers, clergymen, literary men, met at these places and discussed the problems of the hour. Thus the author and his public were forced into intimate proximity. If you admired a man's writings you hastened to his coffee-house, where you might hear him holding forth to his own special friends. Perhaps you brought with you a companion. And thus the circle of discipleship grew.

What the tavern had been to the sixteenth century, the coffee-house was to the seventeenth and eighteenth. It reached the height of its popularity in the eighteenth, and before its close had passed into practical oblivion.

The well-known writers of the day congregated at these places and talked to their friends—not unfrequently *at* them. It was at a coffee-house that Pope found Dryden; and here it was that Addison discoursed to a select circle, and Johnson delivered many of his sententious periods.

The Rise of Journalism.—The earliest newspapers were voluminous concerns. The first circulating in London was the *Mercurius Gallobelgicus*, a bound book of 625 pages, written in

Latin and printed at Cologne. It was concerned with the story of the German Wars. Gradually the identification of a particular paper with a definite political or social philosophy was possible, and in 1695 the Censorship of the Press was abolished and the publication of a modern newspaper became practicable.

The Tatler started by detailing news mingled with essays and stories and dramatic criticism. It was through the influence of Addison that the essay became the most important constituent.

January 2, 1711, saw the death of *The Tatler*, and the following March 1, the birth of *The Spectator*. It ran for 555 numbers, continuing until December 6, 1712. The essay, which had proved so great a success in *The Tatler*, became the one ingredient of *The Spectator*. The sobriety and moderation displayed by the writers, the humour, the genial moralising, these qualities made for the stupendous success of the Journal.

The *Essays* of Addison mirror the life of the time in much the same way as did Chaucer's *Canterbury Tales*. We come across the needy versifier, Ned Softly, frequenting the coffee-house to find an audience for his verses; the happy-go-lucky vagrant Will Wimble; Will Honeycomb; the elderly Tom Rake, and most vital and lovable of all, the genial country squire, Sir Roger de Coverley. In fact here in its pictures of the Town are all the materials of the modern Novel of social life.

Daniel Defoe.—To many people Defoe is chiefly known as the author of *Robinson Crusoe* (1719), and a few other tales dealing with low life. And yet, fiction was merely an incident in Defoe's astoundingly varied career. He was fifty-eight when he wrote *Robinson Crusoe*, and before that time he had been—a merchant, a manufacturer, a satirist, a public official, and an editor.

In 1706 appeared *The True Relation of the Apparition of one Mrs. Veal*, and here he gave proof of his power to create that illusion of reality which is the mainspring of successful fiction, and which he employed with finer results later on in *Robinson Crusoe* (1719) and subsequent experiments in fiction—that vivacious portrait of a pirate, *Captain Singleton* (1720), *Moll Flanders* (1721), *Colonel Jack* (1722), and *Roxana* (1724), dealing with the shadier side of London life; and the admirably realistic make-believe *Journal of the Plague Year* (1722).

His work is characterised by an intensely concrete imagination, and a remarkable aptitude for manipulating detail. What makes *Robinson Crusoe* so remarkable a book is the fine touch of precision which he imparts to the story by his clear, matter of-fact manner.

Why do boys take *Robinson Crusoe* so warmly to their hearts? Because he gives exactly those matters which the boy is curious about—*i.e.* how many biscuits he ate, how he built the raft, what the parrot talked about. Nor are the details overdone. Defoe could make an inventory as appetising as Scott could an adventure. His power of giving dramatic value to detail is well seen in the *Journal of the Plague Year*—*e.g.* where the piper is carried off in the dead-cart.

Underlying the fiction and pamphlets alike there is a clear, satirical purpose—to expose the pretences and social ills of the day. In his pictures of low life he draws attention to the terrible effect of bad environment, and in such a pamphlet as *Poor Man's Plea* (*c.* 1698), he attacked with a vigour which Mr. Blatchford could not have bettered, the injustice of the laws against immorality, and the distinction made between the treatment of rich and poor.

As a writer he helped to kill the high-falutin romance, so long a favourite; and while his lack of imaginative depth and tenderness give pronounced limitations to his work, and his didacticism is often oppressive, yet with obvious failings he combines considerable and often underrated merits. He was fair-minded and good-hearted, no small matter in those days; a good fighter, who fought honestly in the open, and if his ideals were not very inspiring, he never pretended they were: a sincere, just, kindly, unaffected man.

JONATHAN SWIFT was a keen and passionate political partisan, who wrote first for the Whigs, afterwards for the Tories. In an age of famous and brilliant pamphleteers he is second to none. But he is more even than this; he is one of the greatest satirists in English literature. Political and social life are thrown into the crucible of his wrath, and there emerged—the mocking allegory, *Gulliver's Travels*.

His first prose piece, *The Dissensions of Athens and Rome* (1701) (with due application to current politics), has no special merits. In the *Battle of the Books* (1704) he is clear, brilliant, and apposite; and in *The Tale of a Tub*[1] (1704) his satirical power is at its height.

Gulliver's Travels (1726) is richer in content and wider in its appeal, and in *Drapier's Letters* (1724) (with reference to the coinage); the *Polite Conversation* (1738) (concerning the ways of "good" society); and *Directions to Servants* (a side picture on

1 In olden times a discursive story was called the "Tale of a Tub."

the manners of the age), we have admirable illustrations of his pungent wit and stinging irony.

What is the special quality of Swift's satire, and how does it differ from his contemporaries?

In certain respects Swift resembles Defoe. There is direct vigour and matter-of-factness about his satire, and like Defoe, he uses irony to drive home a point. Less wide in his range than Defoe, and more savage in his methods, he sounds profounder depths, and exhibits a more cosmic humour than his contemporary. The humour is often as bitter as gall, but its power and appositeness are beyond question. Tragedy is written across Swift's life. His intellectual audacity stood in his own pathway. There could be no preferment for the Churchman who so mercilessly ridiculed theology in *The Tale of a Tub;* no happiness for a lover so capricious and incalculable as he; no content for a man who, in an age when the emotional life was kept so sternly subjected, looked out upon life with such fierce and passionate intensity of feeling. He is like a man born out of due time; and though he stands alone among the men of his age, unable to endure the easy cynicism of men like Gay, who held life to be a jest, or to follow the genial humanity of Steele and graceful urbanities of Addison, yet he was not great enough to rise above them. On the critical side he is supremely great; none could despise the world and mankind with such brilliant fury. But he had no alternative; nothing to put in the place of material ambition. He is at heart as worldly as Defoe; and it is part of his tragedy that he recognises the fact.

Among lesser names of the time, as makers of prose, are Dr. John Arbuthnot, the great-hearted friend of Swift, of whom Swift said, "If the world had but a dozen Arbuthnots in it, I would burn my travels." He was a noted physician, a ripe scholar, a wit who would hold his own with the best of his contemporaries. As a writer he lacked the integrity and originality of the great prose men; followed frankly the literary methods of Swift, avoiding the bitterness, and did much to popularise his master by drawing attention to his genius. Bolingbroke, a brilliant political and social figure in his own age, has little literary significance to-day.

He had a nimble wit and a facile pen, but was fundamentally insincere, and his flashy talent was not considerable enough to impart vitality to his writing. Sharply contrasting with him is the figure of the Irishman, GEORGE BERKELEY, a man of subtle intellect and noble character. His chief works are

Theory of Vision (1709), *The Principles of Human Knowledge* (1710), and Dialogues between *Hylas and Philonous* (1713) (in which the materialist and idealist standpoint are discussed), *Alciphron, or the Minute Philosopher* (1732), in which his metaphysics is stated with rare dialectical skill, and in a singularly lucid and graceful style. According to Pope, Berkeley had been vouchsafed "every virtue under heaven"; and although his theory that matter is illusory, and that what we see and handle is merely symbolic of spiritual realities, met with a good deal of ridicule from the "common-sense" school of the day, yet no man was better praised or in greater favour than he. Few thinkers indeed have had such command of literary expression. In his moral ideas he curiously foreshadows much of the modern school of economics—*i.e.* "Whether the four elements and man's labour therein be not the true source of wealth." "Whether pictures and statues are not in fact so much treasure."

If Berkeley anticipates the modern school of economists, so did Mandeville in his *Fable of the Bees* (1714) anticipate the criticism of political society, which started with Godwin and still continues in the hands of Edward Carpenter and Bernard Shaw. *The Fable of the Bees* is partly in verse, partly in prose, and has as its thesis the innate corruptness of modern civilisation.

IV

THE AGE OF SENSE AND SENSIBILITY (*c.* 1740–80)

Johnson and the Eighteenth Century Novelists

1. Dr. Johnson and his Circle

Characteristics of the later Eighteenth Century.—There is a real difference between the psychological atmosphere of Dryden's day and that of Johnson's. Differences of this kind are not to be sharply defined by chronological means, for the satirical brilliance that came into vogue with the Restoration lasted on until the publication of the *Dunciad* (1728). Meanwhile, however, during the later years of Pope, a more sober habit of mind began to prevail, and sensibility, so long ruled out of literature, broke the literary barriers with a vengeance.

Four years before the death of Pope, a generation that had acclaimed his polished unemotional verse, went mad over the riotous sentimentality of Richardson's *Pamela* (1740).

Good Sense plus greater Sensibility—e.g. Pope and Johnson.—Good sense is as characteristic of Dryden as of Johnson. Yet we are conscious of some change. What is it? It is the advent of sensibility—an emotional sensitiveness, that soon found expression in literature, and gradually merged into the larger and deeper imaginative life of the Romantic Revival.

One of the commonplaces of literary criticism is an insistence on the matter-of-fact, unemotional character of the eighteenth century, for three-quarters at any rate of its span. The generalisation has this element of truth in it, that nearly all the verse, and much of the drama is, as we have seen, intellectual rather than emotional, critical rather than imaginative, satirical rather than passionate. But it was, after all, only a literary convention which held the field for a while.

The English people were no less emotional or sentimental in Pope's day than they were in Shelley's or in Shakespeare's.

Dr. Johnson.—Samuel Johnson more than any other figure sums up in his person the general characteristics of his time; its vigorous didacticism and awakened sensibility. Dr. Johnson lives rather as a personality than as an author, for despite the sound criticism that scintillates from time to time in the ponderous *Lives of the Poets* (1779–81), the flashes of beauty in his novel *Rasselas* (1759), and the rough genial humour that illuminates his Essay work in the *Idler* and *Rambler*, he ranks as a writer on a lower level than the majority of the men who form his circle, in every department which he essayed; his prose has neither the vitality of Fielding, the charm of Goldsmith, the splendour of Gibbon, or the eloquence of Burke. Yet as a personality he surmounts them all, and was looked upon as the guide and leader of his brilliant coterie.

His Characteristics: Sense, Tenderness, Humour, Humanity.—Without the illuminating discipleship of Boswell, it would be hard for us to account for this fact, but his biographer has supplied the key. And we realise to-day that the best part of Johnson never found literary expression, but lives in his table-talk. His strong sense, his unfailing tenderness, his rough, contrary but wholesome humour;—in short, the sturdy humanity of the burly Dictator; these are the things which make Johnson's name alive to-day.

Few better things were said of him than the grateful tribute of Goldsmith: "He has nothing of him of the bear but the skin."

Goldsmith compared with Johnson.—Oliver Goldsmith presents a striking contrast both in his person and work. As a personality, his quaint, inconsequential manner and naïve simplicity—which not even the harsh school of experience could alter—compare strongly with Johnson's authoritative dogmatism and worldly wisdom. As a writer, what could be more unlike the massive pomposity of Johnson than the clear, delicate, and limpid style of Goldsmith? Working always under heavy disabilities, he has left us *The Vicar of Wakefield* (1766), a novel which, of its kind, has become a classic; a body of verse, notably *The Traveller* (1764), and *The Deserted Village* (1770), of great sweetness and charm; two comedies, *The Good-Natur'd Man* (1768) and *She Stoops to Conquer* (1773), one of which still holds the stage; and *Essays*, after the *Spectator* fashion, of the highest quality. He is a poet of talent: a prose writer of genius. The Essays in *The Citizen of the World* show a play of fancy and a whimsical humour shot with pathos, that place them beside the best work of Leigh Hunt, and all but the best work of "Elia."

Edmund Burke.—Edmund Burke is another of the Johnson circle, and like his fellow-countryman, Goldsmith, came over also from Ireland to try his fortune in London. There is a warmth and colour about his style, which we shall not find in any other prose-man of the day; though it has to be remembered that he was an orator first, and rhetorical methods conditioned his prose from first to last. His study in æstheticism, *Inquiry into the Origin of our Ideas of the Sublime and Beautiful*, secured him in 1757 an introduction to Johnson. This and his *On Causes of the Present Discontents* (1770) are his most important contributions to literature.

Historians: Hume, Robertson, and Gibbon.—Historical writing is raised into literary importance by *David Hume*, *Dr. Robertson*, and *Edward Gibbon*. Of these three, Gibbon is unquestionably the greatest, for although in common with the others he is lacking in sympathetic insight, he has greater imaginative force and a more considerable knowledge. His monumental *Decline and Fall of the Roman Empire* (1776–88), if wanting in the flexibility and warmth which we find in Burke, is at its best eloquent and impressive.

Philosophy and Social Politics.—In the realm of Philosophy and Social Politics we have Hume's *Treatises on Human Nature* (1739), in which, following Locke, he limits knowledge to phenomena cognisable by experience; and Adam Smith's *Wealth of Nations* (1776), postulating labour as the source of wealth. The Evangelical Revival and the work of *Wesley* and *Whitefield* gave literary significance to some of the devotional writings of the time, notably the *Sermons* of Dr. Chalmers, but on the whole the philosopher and the theologian of the eighteenth century show but little grace of style or charm of manner.

In the miscellaneous literature of the day mention must be made of Sir Joshua Reynolds' pleasant *Discourses on Painting* (1769–90), and the light, amusing touch of Horace Walpole's *Letters*.

2. The Novel

The sensibility that marked the later years of the eighteenth century, though amply reflected in Johnson's personality, finds its fullest literary expression in the fiction that sprang of a sudden into popularity. The common-sense ideal haunts the novel no less than the essay, and is especially emphasized in Fielding's outlook on life; but there are many indications to show a rising in the temperature of our emotional and imaginative life.

Despite the promising start made by prose fiction in the sixteenth century, the stir of new and distracting social interests in the seventeenth proved unfavourable to the development of the novel.

But the work of the Diarists, of John Bunyan's Allegories, the rise of English Journalism—all these literary forms which fostered and encouraged pictures of current life and manners, helped forward the novel. And when the Drama began to decline in popularity, the Novel stepped into its place.

To that enterprising journalist, Defoe, must be accorded the honour of pioneering the new fiction of contemporary actualities. Defoe's fiction, however, had two great defects—lack of sentiment and lack of humour. The new school of novelists speedily made those deficiencies.

Richardson and the Sentimental Note.—Samuel Richardson followed Defoe in dealing with contemporary life, but suffused his scenes with a sentimental pathos which promptly took the town. This tubby, mild-mannered little man, who lived the life of an industrious tradesman, with less stuff of adventure in the whole of his career than Defoe had in a few months, became the idol of the hour, and moved in an adoring crowd of sobbing female worshippers. How account for his amazing popularity?

Largely, because he had a ready instinct for woman's ways. From early days he had studied the sex, and had once written love letters for some young women; and in an age when sentiment had been shut outside the garden of poesy, and eschewed so rigorously in much of the prose, its sudden entrance into fiction was hailed by many with delight. It is not easy to find the virtue in *Pamela, or Virtue Rewarded* (1740), but its sentimentality brims over, and mawkish as it may seem to the modern reader, it was avidly swallowed by the readers of the day.

Richardson followed this up by a more legitimate appeal to the emotions in *Clarissa Harlowe* (1747). So firm an affection did Clarissa and her sorrows evoke, that Colley Cibber swore if she should die he would no longer believe in Providence. His last novel, *Sir Charles Grandison* (1754), is of extraordinary length, even in an age of lengthy fiction; but despite this, its utter lack of humour, and the priggishness of the eighteenth-century egoist, Sir Charles, it contains some skilful analysis of character. Sentimental analysis is a commonplace in modern fiction. But Richardson was its first exponent. Prolix and artificial to a degree, in style, the discerning reader will realise genuine observation and real emotional power beneath all the verbiage and egregious sentimentalities. And therein lies the secret of his power. Sterne, Fanny Burney, and even Jane Austen show traces of his influence; while Diderot and De Musset in France, and Goethe in Germany, testify to his power.

Fielding and the Humorous Note.—If to Richardson we owe the note of sentiment, dashing and versatile Henry Fielding may claim to have imported the note of humour. Starting as a parodist of Richardson in his *Joseph Andrewes* (1742), he soon discovered his own powers in *Tom Jones* (1749), a novel as superior in constructive power to Richardson's as it is in its genial and tolerant outlook on life. In analytical force and subtlety he is inferior to his contemporary, but his was the fresher and more vigorous mind. He attempted to paint a faithful picture of human life as he saw it, and in reproducing the broad features of town and country life in the mid-eighteenth century he is unsurpassed.

Fielding's full-blooded humour and his inventive faculty are best shown in his two early novels. In his last, *Amelia* (1751), the underlying tenderness in his nature finds ampler outlet. Here, also, his powers of satire are more finely and keenly displayed. None of his novels so fully exhibit his satiric genius, however, as does his life of that arch rogue, *Jonathan Wild* (1743).

While Richardson and Fielding were at the height of their

fame, Tobias Smollett published his first novel, *Roderick Random* (1748). Like Fielding, he was considerably influenced in the form of his work by the Spanish picaresque novel.

In constructive power, Smollett falls far behind Fielding; but in descriptive power he is fully as vital and arresting. In experience of life, Smollett had the advantage. English rural society, and aristocratic society, are better known to Fielding; but Smollett's years in Scotland and his knowledge of the "*nautical* multitude," provided him with material to which Fielding could lay no claim. In his own day he was vastly popular, and Scott put him on a level with Fielding. In our own day his reputation has certainly declined, probably because of the more limited range of his appeal. As a literary artist he is, on the whole, inferior to Richardson, Fielding, Sterne, and Goldsmith. But for infectious high spirits, and in the depiction of oddities, he has no equal save Dickens. As for his sea worthies, they are inimitable—over-coloured maybe, but abounding in life and prodigal in comic invention.

Tom Bowling in *Roderick Random*, and Hawser Trunnion in *Peregrine Pickle*, to say nothing of Hatchway and Pipes, have the salt savour of the sea about them.

His best book is *Humphry Clinker* (1771). Lacking the animal spirits of its predecessors, it is the richest in humorous observation of character.

Laurence Sterne revives the sentimental art again, though with a lighter touch.

Symmetry and cohesion are flung to the winds.

Sterne and the Note of Subtlety.—There is no more chaotic novel in literature than *Tristram Shandy* (1760); and *A Sentimental Journey* (1768) is little better. But the leisurely *Tristram Shandy* is one long parenthesis; a colossal aside. Yet the chaos is intentional, the incoherence deliberate. It is a trick to arrest the reader, and certainly succeeds. Sterne's frank and impudent neglect of form—his buttonholing pose; his inconsequential confidences, are undeniably attractive; for behind it all there is the humorist of fine sensibility, the subtle artist.

Here is a fair specimen of Sterne's humour:

"It was a consuming vexation to my father, that my mother never asked the meaning of a thing she did not understand. 'That she is not a woman of science,' my father would say, 'is her misfortune; but she might ask a question.' My mother never did. In short, she went out of the world, at last, without knowing whether it turned round or stood still. My father had officiously told her above a thousand times which way it was, but she always forgot."

This sly, evasive humour is quite other than the breezy robustiousness of Fielding or the exuberant extravagance of Smollett, while the creation of Uncle Toby and the wonderful little scene with the Ass of Lyons, are in themselves sufficient to vindicate Sterne's genuine though fitful faculty for pathos.

Goldsmith.—The Idyllic Note.—Goldsmith's *Vicar of Wakefield* (1766) is in very different manner. Goldsmith succeeds by virtue of his exquisitely lucid style and simple humanity.

The *Vicar* triumphs not because of any special outstanding quality—Goldsmith derives something from each of his predecessors—but through its pervasive idyllic charm.

The Women Novelists.—Frances Burney's *Evelina* (1778) gives us a picture of fashionable eighteenth-century life from the woman's point of view. And in its more limited way, *Evelina* is as typical of its time as is *Tom Jones.*

Miss Burney may be remembered, moreover, as the first woman novelist of any considerable distinction.

Mrs. Radcliffe and others who wrote fiction during the closing years of the century belong in style and treatment to the next age. They were forerunners of the Romantic movement. And the last woman writer to carry on the traditions of the eighteenth century is Scott's youthful contemporary, JANE AUSTEN. Living during the early years of the Romantic movement, she was completely untouched by any side of it. More truly even than Frances Burney is she the feminine contemporary of Fielding; and her strong sense of humour kept her from the sentimental absurdities that abound in the eighteenth-century novelists. Faithful observation, personal detachment from her subject and a delicate sense of ironic comedy are Jane Austen's chief characteristics as a writer. The daughter of a country rector, and brought up in the quiet backwater of a small provincial town, Steventon in Hants, her life was singularly uneventful. For most of her time she lived at home; her longest journey was to Bath, her most exciting experience, probably, private theatricals. No serious love attachment is gathered about her; she was a good daughter and sister; a writer from sheer love of writing. Like Charlotte Brontë she was a story-teller from a child. In person tall and graceful, with good features and curly brown hair; in disposition serene, gentle, unemotional, and drily humorous. She wrote seven novels, *Pride and Prejudice* (1813), *Northanger Abbey* (1798), *Sense and Sensibility* (1811), *Mansfield Park, Emma,* and *Persuasion* (1814–16).

One, *Lady Susan*, was never published. There was also a fragment, *The Watsons*, never finished. The material at her hand was not promising; the gossip and scandal of a little country town, where tea-time was a crisis in one's life, and a subscription ball a turning-point in one's career; when adventure expresses itself in country walks (usually with a chaperon), and tragedy hinged upon the non-appearance of that agreeable young man who danced so well at the ball. And yet while no writer is freer from dullness, no story-teller impresses us with such a sense of ease and delicate tact as she. She knew her limitations, and never went outside them. And within her narrow limits she is supreme. She made of tattle a fine art. Tennyson expressed the sentiments of many when he said at Lyme Regis, "Don't talk to me of the Duke of Monmouth! Show me where Louisa Musgrove fell."

V

THE ROMANTIC REVIVAL (*c.* 1780–1832)

Introduction.—No label can accurately describe a period so rich and varied in achievement as the fifty years following the death of Johnson. Yet, while allowing for those distinctive qualities that a genius gives to, rather than takes from an age, there will be found certain underlying characteristics linking the writers of the period together in a masonic brotherhood.

What is Romanticism? What is this emotional tide which ebbs and flows throughout literary history; reaching high-water mark in the age of Shakespeare and of Wordsworth, yet taking on so varying a complexion in the work, say, of a Marlowe or a Scott?

Romanticism surely is a widening of the imaginative horizon, a sharpening of emotional sensibility. At its onset it drives those who feel its spell into strange by-paths of thought and feeling away from the broad highway of ordinary human experience. It was thus with Marlowe in his world-moving visions; thus with Scott in his fervent mediævalism.

But ultimately it brings us back to the highway—only at a greater elevation. We seek it first in the thunder and the earthquake of the fantastic and bizarre, and find it after all in the still small voice of everyday life. In other words, Romanticism is not opposed to Reality. It is Reality transfigured by new powers of vision and feeling. In the deep sense of the word, Marlowe and Scott are realists because of their Romanticism. Marlowe hinted at it in his *Edward II*, though he died too young to realise its full implication. Scott realised it perfectly in his faithful pictures of Scottish life and character.

Stated simply and generally, the features most insistent at this period are, *the spiritualising of Nature* and *the humanising of Social Life.*

The supreme Romantic movement in English letters was the Renascence. It had transformed not only English but European life ; but like every great impulse in Art and Life, it had been followed by a period of reaction. The great Romanticists were, as I have said, also realists, but among the lesser spirits romanticism always generates a certain tendency to exaggeration and aloofness from the conditions of ordinary life. It was the business of the common-sense unimpassioned school that followed to correct these defects. This it accomplished, and it bequeathed to English literature a greater clarity, a closer correspondence with the actualities of life ; and then in its turn becoming artificial and one-sided, another tidal movement was needed for purposes of spiritual adjustment.

The Romantic Revival was the result of no one cause. Broadly speaking, it was the inevitable corollary of the Renascence and Reformation. The dignity and importance of man as man, the glories of the world of nature, these ideas, of which we hear so much at the close of the eighteenth century, were born centuries before, and had been gradually working in men's minds through all the political unrest of the seventeenth and eighteenth centuries. The first flowering of Romanticism in England, the bloody horrors of the French Revolution, the kindling of a new idealistic philosophy in Germany under Kant and Hegel, the political upheaval in America, all these things were but varying symptoms of a general fermentation that had lasted on from the fifteenth century.

It is well to remember this, for although the social theories of Rousseau, roughly embodied in the familiar phrase, the "return to nature," did materially affect doctrinaires like William Godwin, and through Godwin, Shelley; and although the battle-cry of the Revolutionaries, "Liberty, Equality, and Fraternity," impressed itself on the youthful imagination of Wordsworth and Coleridge, the general characteristics of the Revival suggested above were collateral with the Revolution, not derived from it. They arose, as we may see, in verse and fiction during the lifetime of Pope, and impressed many an imagination long before the overthrow of the Bastille had given these ideas a more urgent vitality.

As regards the passion for Nature, so insistent among the poets and certain story-tellers of the time, this may be said. It is not that men like Wordsworth and Shelley cared for Nature *more* than did Shakespeare, or in our own time Tennyson, but they cared in a *different* way. Wordsworth found brooding and tranquillising thought at the heart of Nature. Shelley an ardent and persuasive love—in other words, they spiritualised Nature. To Shakespeare the primrose was a pretty yellow flower, and "nothing more." To Tennyson, the landscape was an exquisite stage property, in which human emotions might be pictorially framed. Shakespeare, with the hearty objectivity of his age, loved Nature without questioning how and wherefore. Tennyson, with the introspective tendency of his age, put his sentiment under the microscope, and found that modern science had stripped Nature of her pontifical robe of metaphysics.

The Spiritualising of Nature.—Now this spiritualising of Nature started as early as Thomson's *Seasons;* it is as yet more implicit than explicit, but as we proceed, growing clearer through the verse of William Collins and Gray; until in Burns, Blake, and Cowper it is exultant in note, and only awaits the shaping imagination of Wordsworth and his great contemporaries to give it consummate artistic expression.

It was because many thought they saw in mediævalism a richer inspiration for the mysterious forces they felt about them, that they turned from modern conditions of life towards the folk-lore and legendary wealth of the Middle Ages. Only gradually did they realise that to find this element of wonder and strangeness, they need not delve in the remote past. It was at their hand. It arose from the natural simplicity which they lauded—the mysticism of everyday life, the magic of the Earth, the witchery of the Seasons.

An ordinary sunset, the garrulity of an old seaman, the rain-bearing wind, the song of a nightingale; these are the things that inspire to great achievement a Wordsworth, a Coleridge, a Shelley, a Keats.

The Humanising of Social Life.—The other feature of the time is closely connected with the heightened appreciation of natural beauty, for it impelled an attraction towards simple and elemental qualities everywhere. This made for the humanising of life, and gave warmth and tenderness, and imaginative sensibility to both the poetry and prose of the age.

1. Poetry

In dealing with the poetry of the time, so abundant in quantity as well as rich in quality, it will be convenient to treat of it around these three dominant personalities: Wordsworth, Scott, and Shelley.

The earliest forerunners of the Romantic Revival were James Macpherson, with his version of the old Celtic legend of *Ossian* (1762), and Bishop Percy, whose collection of old ballads, *Reliques of Ancient Poetry*, appeared in 1764. These two writers stimulated interest in ancient ballad verse and legend, and prepared the way for the precocious Chatterton with his ballad imitations. Then comes Blake, who expressed in his *Songs of Innocence* (1789) both the mysticism and the homely delight of common things; and thus is godfather both to *The Ancient Mariner* and Wordsworth's pastoral domesticities.

The same love of simple joys animates the work of Cowper. These two poets foreshadow the work of the Wordsworthian group, and hint at the kinship with all sentient things which is the link uniting Wordsworth and Shelley.

William Wordsworth.—A quiet, uneventful life spent partly in the south-west of England, but chiefly among the English Lakes. There were two influences in his poetic life; that of his friend Coleridge, which led to the joint production of the famous *Lyrical Ballads* in 1798, and that of his sister Dorothy. The first was the more considerable, the latter the more persistent. Otherwise no poet has proved less susceptible to the influence of other minds than Wordsworth. When quite a youth, the beauty of a sunrise stirred within him a sense of his calling, to be "a dedicated spirit" to Nature. And Nature never had a more faithful devotee.

The matter of the universe was for Wordsworth merely the vesture of a great spiritual power interpenetrating Nature; a rock, a flower, a sunset, a mountain torrent, the beauty of a girl, were for him varying manifestations of this unifying principle. This is the underlying thought of *Tintern Abbey*.

And this peace he finds everywhere at the heart of Nature, "a central peace subsisting at the heart of endless agitation," which fills the poet's heart with a deep, abiding joy—not the ecstatic rapture of Shelley, but a rich, measured contentment. It is the burden of that autobiographical and philosophic fragment, *The Prelude* (1805).

And thus his love of Nature is transferred to the shepherd and simple dalesmen, and after them to Humanity at large. He is the poet of Man just as Browning is the poet of Men.

Samuel Taylor Coleridge.—Supremely plastic in imagination, and susceptible to every cross-current of emotion, Coleridge differs widely in temperament from Wordsworth, with his emotional frugality and steady oneness of vision.

In no other poet of the time is the sense of mystery more finely developed. His mastery of rhythm and metre gave an art which is almost artless in its naïve magic, to the old ballad measure of *The Ancient Mariner* (1798). And in reproducing the ghostly atmosphere of mediæval romance, he is unequalled in our literature. Rossetti alone can approach him with any measure of success. Scott, so adept in dealing with the human elements of mediævalism, failed in reproducing its supernaturalism, both in his verse and prose.

The years of Coleridge's best poetry are from 1794 to 1800. After that the tenuous but precious stream of his poesy dried up; and for the remaining thirty years it is to the metaphysician, critic, and brilliant discursive talker of Highgate Hill that we look. His early verse is turgid and imitative of the eighteenth-century models. But the comradeship of Wordsworth had a quick ripening effect on his genius.

The most remarkable thing about *The Ancient Mariner* and *Christabel* is the mingling of the mystical quality with a stark simplicity of phrasing. What could at once be more homely and more imaginative than these lines:

> "The moving moon went up the sky
> And nowhere did abide;
> Softly she was going up
> And a star or two beside."

The Poetry of Lowly Life.—In dealing with scenes of lowly life, Crabbe had as forerunner William Shenstone with his *Schoolmistress* (1742). He was succeeded by Bloomfield, who wrote *The Farmer Boy* (1798); Ebenezer Elliott, the vigorous and picturesque *Corn Law Rhymer*; and John Clare, author of *Poems Descriptive of Rural Life* (1820).

In imaginative power, George Crabbe is greatly inferior to either Wordsworth or Coleridge, but he had fully as vivid a sense of the richness of everyday life, and a ready faculty for describing simply, unpretentiously, and truly, the lives of the poor, in *The Parish Register* (1807), and *Tales in Verse* (1812).

Scott and his School.—Passing to the Scott group of Poets, we realise that here we have to deal with a more definitely historical atmosphere. As a forerunner of Scott there is Allan Ramsay, the friend of Pope, who wrote simply and feelingly about Scottish life.

Scott, saturated with the Border Minstrelsy, and inspired by Percy's *Reliques*, gives fresh life to the Border Romances in *The Lay of the Last Minstrel* (1805), *Marmion* (1808), and *The Lady of the Lake* (1810). If he lacked the lyric passion of Burns, and the witchery of Coleridge and Keats, he is unexcelled in narrative force and clearness.

Closely identified with Scott are John Leyden, and James Hogg, "The Ettrick Shepherd," and their ballad poetry is rich in imaginative beauty.

The battle chants of William Motherwell, and the stirring war songs of Thomas Campbell, are further memorable additions to the plentiful output of contemporary Scottish verse. What Campbell did for Britain, Thomas Moore achieves for Ireland. He has less force than Campbell, but more sweetness of melody; though posterity has not ratified the high opinion of his contemporaries.

Robert Southey belongs to this group by virtue of his picturesque, historical sense. Not content with exploiting the folk-lore of his country, he pushed Eastward and attained his greatest vogue in dealing with Oriental subjects: *Thalaba* (1801), and *The Curse of Kehama* (1810).

The humblest of the group, though popular enough in their day, are James Montgomery and Mrs. Hemans; they exemplify the spirit of romanticism in its shallowest expressions, though their verse at its best is touched by sweetness and pictorial skill.

Shelley and his Circle.—In the poetry passed under review, the main thing has been the reiteration of the importance of ordinary folk and commonplace things. Those catchwords of the Revolution, Equality and Fraternity, have received varied illustration; but there has been little insistence upon Liberty. Wordsworth and Coleridge, at first enthusiastic in the cause of Revolutionary France, speedily recanted their early faith, and a strong element of conservatism enters into not only their work, but the work of most of their followers and adherents. There is democratic sentiment in Burns, but that of Scott, insistent as it is, affects his prose far more than his verse.

Byron.—When we come to Byron, however, the bolder and freer aspects of Romanticism are to the fore. Lacking the intensity and concentration of Wordsworth, the subtlety of Coleridge, and the sensitive receptivity of Keats, he possessed a breadth of imagination and a caustic wit that gave him a distinctive place among the poets of the age. He shares with his great contemporaries an intense love of Nature, especially in her wilder aspects, and in *Childe Harold* (*c.* 1812), and *The Siege of Corinth* (1815), there are vivid and spirited passages of scenic description.

In style and temperament he is a curious blend of the age of satire and the age of romanticism. There is something of Pope's school in his metrical experiments, something also of the colloquial ease and humour of Dryden in such satirical poems as *English Bards and Scotch Reviewers* (1809). But mingled with this there is the passion for Nature, and his sympathy with the revolutionary spirit.

He has been accused of insincerity, and insincere he could be when he wished. But it was a deliberate insincerity; an actor's pose. And there was a certain elemental greatness in the man despite the limelight attitudinising. In that strange mixture of worldly wisdom and poetic beauty, *Don Juan* (1819), we see Byron at his best. His songs lack the delicacy of Shelley's, but they have a fine lilt and music of their own, and

"She walks in beauty like the night
Of cloudless clime and starry skies"

will take its place among the best lyrics of our literature.

Percy Bysshe Shelley.—Shelley is emphatically the poet of eager, sensitive youth; not the animal youth of Byron, but the spiritual youth of the visionary and reformer. In his earlier years Godwin was the figure who most readily impressed his mobile imagination, and in many of the poems dealing with social subjects—*Queen Mab* (1813) and the *Revolt of Islam* (1818)—he is little more than Godwin made musical. In later life Wordsworth's influence is more clearly discernible. But the most potent inspiration came from Greek literature, first brought before his notice by his kindly friend and critic, Peacock.

Shelley, like his admirer Browning, needed the sunshine of the South to rouse his finest powers. *Alastor* (1816) is the splendid product of his first acquaintance with the Alps; and his loveliest lyrics were written under Italian skies.

Two notes dominate all Shelley's work, epic, narrative, and lyric alike—his devotion to liberty, and his wholehearted belief in love, as the prime factor in all human progress. The Revolution to Shelley was much more than a political upheaval; it was a spiritual awakening, the beginning of a new life. All that was evil in life he traced to Slavery. Natural development for him was the only development. He believed that men would never be men, never give what was best in them until they could give it out freely. Master yourself, he cries, and external freedom will enable you to realise your utmost capabilities. These are the thoughts underlying *The Revolt of Islam*, *The Masque of Anarchy*, *Julian and Maddolo*, and the noble lyric drama *Prometheus Unbound*. Liberty, in Shelley's eyes, was freedom from external restraint. It is opposed to licence, for to "rule the Empire of Self" was with Shelley a moral necessity. What then, if force is withdrawn from Society, is to take its place? Shelley's answer is, Love. Love is to reign supreme, for only in an atmosphere of love can liberty efficiently work. Love is with Shelley a transcendental force kindling all things into beauty. In his treatment of it we miss the more concrete touch of Keats, and the homeliness of Wordsworth's steady affection. And there are times when his dream pictures float away, like exquisite bubbles, that melt even as we watch them.

But both the strength and weakness of Shelley's verse lie in the fact that his fine idealism, and warm human sympathies, are clad in shadowy fantasies, and lyrics delicate as gossamer. Thought and feeling are etherealised, till their presence is discerned only as one discerns the things of dreamland. He is the Oberon of poets; and even in his most impassioned songs, in such matchless lyrics as *The World's great age begins anew*, where our rough guttural tongue becomes an exquisite lyric cry—even here it is as if some fairy child were lamenting the sins and cruelties of mankind: Oberon turned Social Reformer. Whatever may be the fate of his longer poems, his lyrics are sure to live so long as rhythmic beauty and elfin music appeal to humankind.

John Keats.—Keats has more imaginative affinity with Coleridge than with Shelley, and has the same Celtic blood in his veins. The formative influences in his work are the mediæval Italian verse of Leigh Hunt, the pastoral sweetness of Spenser, and the inspiration of Greek art first gained through the medium of Chapman's *Homer*. But his individual genius, though shaped by these influences, soon placed him among the foremost names of his age, while in certain directions he is pre-eminent. The naturalism of Wordsworth's School is blended here with an extraordinary delicacy of observation, which gives his scenic pictures a unique charm. For instance:

> "A little noiseless noise among the leaves,
> Born of the very sigh that silence heaves."

When he first began to write, the wealth of his perceptive life bewildered and embarrassed him. Gradually he found speech, and although an Oriental extravagance of emotion breaks out from time to time, no poet has excelled Keats at his best for splendour of workmanship. *Endymion* (1818), *Isabella* (1818), and *The Eve of St. Agnes* (1819), splendid in colouring as they are, tend to fatigue the eye, because of the excess of ornament. But the *Odes* are among the imperishable things of English verse by virtue of their Hellenic clarity and chiselled beauty, and the poetry comes naturally, as Keats was wont to declare poetry should, "as leaves to a tree." Indeed the thought that inspired him as a poet, the thought condensed into those well-known lines in the *Ode on a Grecian Urn* (1819):

> "Beauty is truth, truth beauty,—that is all
> Ye know on earth, and all ye need to know,"

lies at the very root of Ruskin's teaching, Pater's philosophy, and Morris's social gospel. The insistence on a spiritual principle carried with it new democratic ideals of which probably Keats never thought, but which were to bring literature and life into far more intimate relations; and it seems somewhat strange that the poet, whose work was the most secluded from the rush and turmoil of daily life, should have reminded us so insistently of this eternal fact.

Among the other poets of the romantic revival, belonging especially to this group, are Walter Savage Landor, also profoundly influenced by Greek art. He excels in elaboration of detail and choice sobriety of phrase, but his more characteristic work lies in his *Imaginary Conversations* (1824–29), where his rich, scholarly imagination and exuberant vitality found congenial outlet.

2. The Novel

Just as Macpherson's *Ossian* and Bishop Percy's *Reliques* heralded in the romantic revival in poetry, so did Horace Walpole's *Castle of Otranto* (1764) proclaim its entrance into fiction. The story with its crude supernaturalism is absurd enough. But the essential thing about the book is that it indicated the hankering after romance and mystery which was beginning to beset the writers of the time.

William Beckford, in his Oriental romance *Vathek* (1782), improves upon Walpole in the craftsmanship of "blood-curdling"; and Mrs. Radcliffe, who succeeded, was certainly an artist of considerable graphic power. Her *Mysteries of Udolpho* (1794), with all its extravagances, shows a very genuine appreciation of the sublime and terrible in Nature, and if only for her influence upon such men as Scott and Byron, she deserves the notice of the literary student. It is no exaggeration to say that she brought the passion for Nature, which is so marked a feature of the romantic revival, into English fiction.

In Walpole and Mrs. Radcliffe the background is projected into a past age, but there is no definite historical atmosphere. Romanticism, however, naturally favoured the growth of the historical novel. Moreover, the greater attention given to history in the brilliant work of Gibbon, the pleasant, palatable experiments in this direction of Goldsmith, together with the interest in the past excited by Walpole, made favourably for the production of historical romance, and prepared the way for Sir Walter Scott.

The Note of Mystery and Terror.—The note of mystery and terror which Walpole struck, half in joke, and Mrs. Radcliffe wholly in earnest, was intensified by "Monk" Lewis, and Charles Robert Maturin. Lewis was an expert in the making of horrors, but he is entirely lacking in Mrs. Radcliffe's artistic sincerity. Maturin, an Irish clergyman of French descent, imparts a religious fanaticism into his supernatural horrors. His most ambitious work was *Melmoth the Wanderer* (1820). In *The Frankenstein* (1817) of Mary Shelley, we find supernaturalism and philosophic speculation blended. This romance is a bridge between the pure romance of the Radcliffe school and the doctrinaire romantic novels of William Godwin. In Godwin's *Caleb Williams* (1794), *St. Leon* (1799), and *Fleetwood* (1804), there are distinct traces of the school of mystery and terror, combined with much severely logical reasoning, largely inspired by Rousseau's education theories.

Among his successors we have Mrs. Opie, whose *Adeline Mowbray, or the Mother and Daughter* (1804), is influenced by Godwin; and Mrs. Inchbald, with her *Simple Story* (1791), and *Nature and Art* (1796)—educational stories of real power.

To this time also belongs Thomas Day's *Sandford and Merton* (1783–89)—a scheme for parents, and incidentally a rule of life for children, more remarkable for earnest purpose than persuasive charm.

The educational novelist who used romanticism to sugar-coat didacticism, culminated in Maria Edgeworth. Unlike her predecessors she had a lively style, and a genuine gift of satire, and in *Castle Rackrent* (1800) she gives a very spirited picture of the Irish life which she knew so well; and her humorous portrayal of character and tenderness of heart moved Scott to enthusiastic praise. He did not trouble much about her theories, but admired her greatly as a painter of Irish national life.

Sir Walter Scott.—Scott is the greatest novelist of the romantic revival, because, while seizing upon the picturesque elements of mediævalism, he does not reject the great tradition of the eighteenth century in the direction of transcript from life. His romanticism is tempered with cool common sense. Why does he write of the past in place of his own age? He does so because his imagination lived naturally in the past. He is an historical novelist by temperament, not by profession. Charles Reade reconstructed the past with the art of a brilliant journalist; Thackeray refashioned it as a sympathetic critic; George Eliot treated it from the scholar's standpoint. Scott simply breathed it; it was part and parcel of his thinking life. The subtler sides of romanticism find more notable expression elsewhere. But no one had a keener sense for the pomp and pageantry of a bygone age.

The first novel appeared in 1814, and for the next sixteen years he held the stage of fiction, publishing twenty-nine stories in all. No other novelist save Dickens appealed to so wide a circle, or more entirely captured the fancy of the day. When asked for his opinion of *Waverley,* Lord Holland said, 'We did not one of us go to bed last night—nothing slept but my gout." All his best work is marked by three characteristics: a genius for vitalising the past, a love of nature, and a sturdy humanity.

Throughout his life he was absorbing the folk-lore of his country, and he exhaled antiquarianism as a flower exhales fragrance. There is therefore about his books a fine atmosphere of improvisation; while his rich and varied knowledge flowed from his pen with the ease and naturalness of fireside gossip. He did not rhapsodise over the past as Gibbon did, or moralise about it, from an eighteenth-century niche, as Johnson had done; he dramatised it, made it live before us. There have been many historical romancers more accurate than he in the externals of his tale; none so true to the inmost spirit of the age he is depicting.

And this delight and relish for the past was warmed by a genuine love of Nature. He loved not merely the institutions of his country, but his country's soil; loved it as a child loves, for its associations: and he told Washington Irving that if he did not see the heather at least once a year, he thought he would die. Yet a beautiful landscape to him meant little without the human touch in it. Sanctify it with some legend or personal association, and he took it to his heart at once.

A Tory in politics, he was a Democrat in feelings. None of his characters are more vital than those racy of the soil. The heroes and heroines are pleasant enough in their way, but it is a shadowy way. The peasants, the antiquarians, the bailies, are exuberant realities. He is a clever painter of historical portraits—*e.g.* Louis XI; and the Homer of Scottish national life.

Scott's Contemporaries.—Two friends of Scott achieved distinction in tales of Scottish life—Susan Ferrier and John Galt.

John Galt was an Ayrshire man, who had travelled abroad and met Byron. His one unequivocal success was *Annals of the Parish* (1821), where his vigour and sense of humour are happily displayed.

Galt did for the Scottish parish what Miss Mitford did for the English village. Each excelled in miniature painting.

Susan Ferrier wrote three novels only: *Marriage* (1818), *The Inheritance* (1824), and *Destiny* (1831), each of which made its mark, but she steadily refused the blandishments of publishers to add to their number. She was born in Edinburgh, and excelled in depicting the lesser Scottish gentry.

Scott's Successors.—Among the more remarkable of Scott's numerous successors in romantic fiction are, William Harrison, who turned history into vigorous melodrama; James Grant, whose *Romance of War* (1846) is a picturesque military novel of no little power; and that prolific writer Bulwer Lytton in his earlier phase.

Apart from the writers of historical romance, there are James Justinian Morier, the author of a vivid picture of Persian life, *Hajji Baba* (1824), which has in it the discursive flavour of *Gil Blas*; and Thomas Love Peacock, the fine scholar and wit, who developed a new vein in fiction in his humorous fantasies —of these *Headlong Hall* (1816), *Nightmare Abbey* (1818), and *Melincourt* (1817) are the happiest. He was the friend of Shelley, and as a literary figure is a piquant blend of the critical, ironic eighteenth century and the fervent romanticism of the early nineteenth.

3. Prose other than Fiction

Criticism and the Essayists.—Burke and Goldsmith to some extent were the forerunners of the prose of the romantic revival—Burke with his sensibility to beauty; Goldsmith with his delicate humour. But one feature of the prose came unheralded and with the suddenness of a tropical sunrise. The effect of romanticism upon the critical faculty was such as to inaugurate a new school of literary appreciation, with which are associated the names of Coleridge, Lamb, De Quincey, and Hazlitt.

Divergent in character and genius, these men were animated by a common ideal. To interpret, through the sympathetic imagination, the literature of an age by the light of its own standards. The new criticism therefore is at once historical and æsthetic—historical, in so far as it judged a man's work relatively to his time; æsthetic, inasmuch as it tried to re-create the work itself, and appreciate it as the expression of an individual temperament. How widely remote is this from the absolute standard of criticism implied in the famous "This will never do . . ." of Jeffrey!

CHARLES LAMB was the first to point out the poetic richness of the Renascence drama at large. Thomas de Quincey showed the way to an appreciation of modern German literature, afterwards amplified on more catholic lines by *Carlyle.* William Hazlitt, in his *Lectures on the English Poets* (1818), pioneered a wider and more interpretative spirit of our national verse, and Coleridge gave the impulse to modern Shakespearean criticism; and he was the first to deal with the whole of Shakespeare's work as the expression of a single mind and temperament.

Despite the fragmentary nature of Coleridge's critical work, his was the greatest mind among his contemporaries. In poetry, he influenced the supernaturalism of Scott and Keats. In criticism, his distinction between the reason (an inward spiritual vision), and the understanding (the criterion of the senses), proved of immense value to the theologians of the age, and both the High and Broad Church movements may claim him as their godfather. Equally valuable was his contention that poetry is opposed not to truth but to science; its aim was not to establish truth, but communicate pleasure. Poetry presented us with the concrete symbol; science tried to analyse and abstract the laws embodied.

Apart from the critical genius of these writers, each of them in his own way gave a fresh charm to the art of the Essay. The lovable personality of *Elia* found an exquisite media in those discursive confidences that saw light in *The London Magazine.* No one could gossip in print more delightfully than he, nor more casually and whimsically convey so much good sense and imaginative sensibility. He is the fantastic philosopher of the commonplace experiences of life: the prince of guides to the byways of thought and feeling.

Thomas de Quincey.—De Quincey's genius as an essayist was on other lines. His range is wider, but his style, though fertile in happy turns of expression, lacks the quaint magic and pensive sweetness of Lamb. His most notable work is the *Confessions of an English Opium Eater* (1821), a fine and poignant piece of imaginative autobiography. His experiments in "impassioned prose"—a kind of prose poetry—are ingenious, and occasionally, as in *The English Mail Coach*, dramatically telling; but on a higher plane is the graphic force of the fragmentary *Revolt of the Tartars*.

William Hazlitt.—William Hazlitt started life as an itinerant young portrait-painter, with a taste for philosophy. He soon gave up the brush—he never gave up painting—and his brilliant audacities in prose have survived his experiments in pigment.

There is something of Rousseau's sentimental garrulousness about Hazlitt, and this increases the human interest of his writings. We may dissent from his conclusions, or take exception to certain moods, but he never bores us.

He was the reverse of a sociable man, rarely showing his qualities of mind to any but one or two chosen souls. "One of the pleasantest things in life," he says, "is going on a journey, but I like to go by myself. I cannot see the wit of walking and talking at the same time."

Hazlitt is the Byron of prose. There is the same immense vitality in the *Table Talk* (1821) and *Spirit of the Age* (1825), the same changeableness of mood, the same salt of humour, and something of the same strange mixture of idealist and cynical man of the world, as we see in *Beppo* and *Don Juan*.

Charles Lamb, with his unerring insight, never failed to see the finer side of Hazlitt. He declared that Hazlitt in a natural and healthy state was the finest and wisest of spirits breathing.

Leigh Hunt.—On a somewhat humbler level is Leigh Hunt, the friend of Shelley and Keats. He took a vigorous part in the politics of his time, but is better remembered for his agreeable verse, inspired by Italian models, which served to stimulate Shelley's *Julian and Maddalo*, and Keats' *Lamia* —for instance *The Story of Rimini* (1816). He had a lively humour, less delicate than Lamb's, but akin to it in whimsical charm, which gives a pleasant quality to his essay work.

The Development of Journalism.—The intense interest in political and social events at the time of the French Revolution found active and instant expression in the great English Journals which came into existence at this time. *The Times*, *The Morning Chronicle*, and *The Morning Post* had started before the close of the eighteenth century; and these were followed during the early years of the new era by the foundation of four famous critical Reviews: *The Edinburgh*, *The Quarterly*, *Fraser's*, and *Blackwood's Magazines*. Some of the greatest men of letters of the day wrote for these; and despite the pontifical character of the big Reviews, and their political bias, productive at times of notoriously unfair sledge-hammer criticism, it would be unjust to lose sight of the critical value of a good deal of their work. Among the most prominent writers are such men as Francis Jeffrey, Sydney Smith, Lord Brougham, Professor Wilson, John Lockhart; while Coleridge, Hazlitt, Southey and Carlyle, and Macaulay, did admirable work for them.

Lighter in kind and more literary in interest were such papers as *The London Magazine* (for which Lamb and De Quincey wrote), and Leigh Hunt's *Examiner*. Later in the century came *The Westminster Review*, largely connected with the work of John Stuart Mill.

VI

THE VICTORIAN ERA (*c.* 1832–1900)

Introduction.—Two strongly marked characteristics affect Victorian life and thought: the growth of the democratic spirit, and the rapid development of scientific ideas.

In the poetry of the time the democratic spirit is reflected in Hood's *Song of the Shirt;* Elizabeth Barrett Browning's *Cry of the Children*, Tennyson's *Locksley Hall*, and the socialistic songs of Charles Kingsley and William Morris. While in the fiction of the age, many of the story-tellers assume the mantle of the Reformer. Social reconstruction is written in big letters right across the voluminous work of Dickens; Mrs. Gaskell, Charlotte Brontë, and "Mark Rutherford" deal with the industrial unrest of the time; Charles Reade tilts furiously against various social abuses; Kingsley preaches the gospel of sanitation; Disraeli paints the political democracy; and Walter Besant directs attention to East London, with his *All Sorts and Conditions of Men*.

The geological discoveries of Sir Charles Lyell, the biological investigations of Robert Chambers, who prepared the way for *The Origin of Species*, of Charles Darwin, for Alfred Russell Wallace, Thomas Huxley, and the philosophic generalisations of Herbert Spencer; all these intellectual streams of thought flowed over into the literature of the age, and profoundly influenced it.

Tennyson treats Nature like an imaginative man of science; Robert Browning is often more like an analytical chemist than an artist; Matthew Arnold and Arthur Hugh Clough are largely occupied with the discrepancies between scientific discovery and religious faith; and although the Pre-Raphaelite School rise in protest against this intellectual invasion of the world of poesy, not even they can quite escape its influence. Among the novelists of the age to voice the scientific spirit, the names of George Eliot, George Meredith, and Thomas Hardy readily occur.

Finally, in comparing the critical prose of the romantic movement with Victorian prose, we may see how the old-world flavour of Lamb is exchanged for the latter-day political strictures of Carlyle. The fantasies of De Quincey give place to the ironic, social commentary of Arnold, and in place of the literary heresies of Hazlitt we get the economic heresies of Ruskin and Morris.

1. Poetry

Tennyson.—There is no poet who more completely reflects in his verse the questions that were agitating the minds of the average Englishman in Victorian times than Alfred Tennyson. When he began to write the great romantic poets had finished their work, and overshadowed by their rich legacy of song, his early work sounds no very authentic note. It is pretty album verse, to which the eighteenth century phrase *elegant* seems applicable. But in the volume of 1842, the superficial prettiness of the early verse is replaced by something much stronger and finer. Such a poem as *Morte d'Arthur* exhibits those qualities of lucidity, melody, and dignity which inform the poet's best work.

In Memoriam is in many ways Tennyson's most noble achievement. There is a greater lyric passion and splendour in its successor, *Maud;* but it combines the gracious dignity of *Morte d'Arthur* with the clarity and precision of his narrative poems and the rhythmic music of his *Idylls*. As a poetic statement of the religious doubts of the time, it obtained a powerful hold over Tennyson's generation. To us to-day, to whom Darwin is not the last word in thought, the exquisite artistry of the poem appeals the more intimately. Tennyson is the poet of average humanity, and in his verse we find the ordinary concerns of life touched by him just as they affect the average man and women. With a considerable measure of Wordsworth's naked power of expression and homeliness of subject-matter, he brings to his pictures of English life a tenderness and caressing grace all his own. His love of ornament leads him into tawdriness at times, just as Wordsworth's love of simplicity makes him trivial. But on his own ground, in dealing with the broad features of our national life—with its passion for domesticity, deep-rooted reverence for the past, and frank insular enthusiasm, he is unexcelled. In his dramatic experiments, in his modern sentimental treatment of the Arthurian Legend, he is not at his best. The beauty of the Arthurian

Legend, so strongly and poignantly treated by Morris, is not well exhibited by being turned into a latter-day "Morality"; and although he showed genuine power of presenting character in monologue in his dialect poems, both he and Browning lacked that essential of good drama—the power of presenting character in action. But as a word-painter of typical English scenery, as the exponent of the simple emotions of everyday life, he has no equal. And all these matters are portrayed with extraordinary delicacy and crystalline clearness. With his deliberate abstention from the violent and unusual, it required great art to avoid bathos. On the whole, Tennyson emerges triumphant from the ordeal. For other poets, the Alpine wonders and the raptures of life; in Tennyson's company we are beside the green pastures and still waters.

Tennyson and Browning as Artists.—As an artist Tennyson's place is secure; and his friend Robert Browning, to whom the thing said was always of more importance than the way of saying it, must take a secondary place. But as an intellectual force shaping and testing the shifting problems of his time, Browning is just as certainly his superior.

Their Literary Methods.—In literary method they have nothing in common. Tennyson is descriptive and panoramic; Browning never essays more than a side view of his subject, and plunges into the middle of his topic at once—

> "Which do you pity the most of us three,
> My friend, or the mistress of my friend
> With her wanton eyes, or me?"

Where Tennyson is deliberate, measured, eclectic, Browning is impulsive, passionate, omnivorous. He is as profoundly interested as Tennyson or Arnold in the conflict between Science and Religion, though unlike them he is stimulated, not depressed by it.

"He has plenty of music in him," said Tennyson of his friend, "but he can't get it out." It was more a case of *wouldn't* than *couldn't*. Browning was a real poet and a great poet. Only a great poet could have given us *Pippa Passes* and *The Ring and the Book*. But he was a great poet by fits and starts; for so interested is he in men and things, that he will throw aside the artist's robe in order to get on more intimate terms with his reader. If he can talk to us in terms of rhythmic beauty, well and good; if not, so much the worse for rhythmic beauty! A large part of Browning's work consists of little novels in verse, and intellectual discussion thrown into some rough metrical mould.

But if often harsh and unmusical, and deliberately obscure, not through vagueness of thought but because he has no regard for the slower-witted reader, he is never negligible. Like Whitman his personality is intensely vital, and of nearly all his writings can one say, "This is no book; who touches this touches a man."

Elizabeth Barrett Browning.—His wife, Elizabeth Barrett Browning, apart from the romantic part she played in her husband's life, chiefly interests us as doing for modern poetry what Charlotte Brontë did for fiction. She was not a great artist, nor an acute thinker, but she had the power of expressing with fine sensibility, passion, and force the woman's point of view. From this standpoint she touches the social problems of her time in *Aurora Leigh,* while her *Sonnets from the Portuguese* (1845) are the finest poems we have of the self-expressed love of a wife and mother. These are her most remarkable contributions to poetry, and may take their place along with Rossetti's *House of Life.*

Arnold and Clough.—The sceptical unrest of the mid-century is forcibly mirrored in Clough's unequal verses, and more fastidiously and exquisitely expressed in the classic art of Arnold. If not a great poet, Arnold was certainly a genuine one within somewhat narrow limits. Wistful suavity rather than strength; delicate irony rather than lyric passion, informs his verse. This suavity is never more happily expressed than in the *Scholar Gipsy* and *Thyrsis,* where Oxford and the Thames are his inspiration. For irony, what better example than the *Obermann* poems? This of the East:

> "She let the legions thunder past,
> And plunged in thought again."

Or for a line of wistful regret:

> "The unplumbed, salt, estranging sea."

Dover Beach, one of his most characteristic poems, reflects the melancholy of a troubled but brave spirit. In short, a fine artist, more limited in his music than Tennyson, less virile and original than Browning; but unexcelled in depicting certain wistful moods of human experience.

Poetry and the Pre-Raphaelite Movement.—In its narrower aspects this was an Art movement that tried to restore to modern painting something of that individuality and sincerity which characterised the painters before Raphael,—*e.g.* Giotto, Bellini, and Fra Angelico. It originated with a book of engravings which Holman Hunt and Millais saw at Rossetti's house, of certain Italian frescoes. And the Brotherhood embodied a protest against the mechanical and superficial art of the day.

In its broader aspects pre-Raphaelitism was a plea for the imaginative life, a protest against the intellectualism which had crept into the poetry of the age, and had threatened its emotional and artistic vitality.

In a sense, therefore, it was a hark back to the earlier romanticism, and mediæval enthusiasm plays certainly a considerable share in its manifestations.

In its broader aspects, moreover, it is related to the Tractarian Movement, which also emphasized the imaginative as opposed to the intellectual life, and was as impatient with modern scientific thought as the pre-Raphaelites themselves. Only whereas the pre-Raphaelite said: Science has nothing to do with art—it is irrelevant; the Tractarian said: Science has nothing to do with religion—it is wrong. To Newman and Keble the scientific "time-spirit" was a moral curse; to Rossetti and Morris merely a nuisance. Religious art bulks largely in their work, but it is the æsthetics, not the dialectics of Christianity that concern them. Rossetti's poetry therefore denotes a break in the poetic traditions of the age.

Dante Gabriel Rossetti.—In two of his poems, *Jenny*, and *The Burden of Nineveh*, he touches certain aspects of modern life; but with this exception his poetry, like that of Keats, is a world apart—a world of mystic beauty and romance.

It must always be remembered Rossetti was half Italian in temperament, and although his fervent love poetry may repel many by its sensuous frankness, it never justified Robert Buchanan's bitter attack. For it is sensuous, not sensual. To the Italian mind the human body is as sacred as the mind, and the senses are sacramental emblems of the spirit. Italian love poetry, therefore, however fevered and voluptuous it may be, is never gross or base; since it does not extol the senses at the expense of the soul, but glorifies the soul through the senses.

Christina Rossetti.—The devout faith of Christina Rossetti removes her from the pagan romanticism of her brother and William Morris. With less variety and depth of passion than Elizabeth Barrett Browning, she is a greater artist. Her work lacks the fundamental brain power of her brother, but has on the whole greater clarity. In two only of Dante Gabriel Rossetti's poems, *The Blessed Damozel* and *My Sister's Sleep*, does he achieve the lucent simplicity of his sister; and in her charming *Goblin Market* she touches a note of fantasy almost Shakespearean in its convincing magic.

The mystic aspects of mediævalism appealed to Rossetti much as they appealed to Coleridge. And if Coleridge and Rossetti approximate in this, so do Scott and William Morris, in preferring the broader and more spectacular side of the life of the Middle Ages.

William Morris.—William Morris was in reality a great artist who wrote verse as one of many media for expressing his innate sense of beauty, for it was certainly a moot point at times whether the outcome of Morris's inspiration would be a poem or a wall-paper. His well-known dictum, that a man who was unable to turn from an epic to a tapestry had better leave both alone, is finely characteristic. He could do either so well that he often merged the one into the other. He wove his epic with the craftsman's cunning, and wrote his stories in coloured silks. His best work in verse reads like happy improvisations, while his unerring instinct for beauty and his mastery of metrical form kept him free from the pitfalls of the fluent rhymester. Even more than Scott, Morris loved the Middle Ages for their human elements; the democratic note is always insistent, and a fundamental sympathy with "simple folk not troubled with the intricacies of life," unites Morris the Poet with Morris the Social Reformer. There is an ease, a naturalness in his narrative work, and in his power to tell a good story in verse, lucidly and simply; he has no equal save Chaucer.

The common criticism of Morris's poetry, that there are no mountain peaks in it, is true enough, but like all negative criticism misses the peculiar beauty of his work. He flies low, purposely, designedly. In keeping close to the earth, as he does in his delightful re-telling of Mediæval, Greek, and Scandinavian stories in *Jason*, *The Earthly Paradise*, *Sigurd*, and *Love is Enough*, Morris provides us with many compensations for the lack of rhythmic felicities in his work; none more welcome than the fresh sweetness and level excellence of his work as a whole.

There is one poetic quality in which the Rossettis and Morris are deficient—lyric power. That quality is supplied by the youngest of the pre-Raphaelite Poets—ALGERNON CHARLES SWINBURNE. He was indeed, as Tennyson happily said, "a reed through which all things blow into music." The appeal of the others had been chiefly to the eye; their art was essentially pictorial. Swinburne, like Shelley, appeals chiefly to the ear. Indeed his music is grander than Shelley's. Shelley's melodies are sweet and simple: Swinburne's complex orchestral effects. *Atalanta in Calydon* took the Victorian world by storm; in its sweeping power and stirring strains it struck an entirely fresh note in the poetry of the time. The publication of *Poems and Ballads*, with its frank eroticism, two years later, checked the chorus of praise. But these were merely literary "wild oats" sown by the youthful poet, and in rhythmic power this book is even greater than its predecessor. The second volume of *Poems and Ballads* finally confirmed the great lyrical reputation of Swinburne. His work touches every key of song from verses light and enchanting as fairy music, such as:

"For a day and a night Love sang to us, played with us,
Folded us round from the dark and the light;
And our hearts were fulfilled of the music he made with us,
Made with our hearts and our lips while he stayed with us,
Stayed in mid passage his pinions from flight
For a day and a night,"

to the sombre splendour of—

"So long I endure, no longer; and laugh not again, neither weep—
For there is no good found stronger than death; and death is a sleep."

Swinburne's is the last word of the romantic reaction. It is pre-Raphaelitism in its most exultant and defiant mood, and with it the era of great Victorian poetry comes to a close.

Of the lesser constellations of the age it is impossible to speak save in the briefest terms. Thomas Hood, of whose serious work mention has been made, made his reputation as a versifier of ingenious comic invention, exhibiting, moreover, a vein of delicate fancy in *The Plea of the Midsummer Fairies*, and a graphic power in his grim *Dream of Eugene Aram.* While Charles Kingsley proved himself a lyric poet of the people, who brought passion and fine sensibility into such songs as *The Three Fishers*, and *The Sands o' Dee.* James Thomson's *City of Dreadful Night* shows the influence of the sceptical tendencies of the day upon a sensitive and morbid mind.

Humour and Satire.—The growth of a more critical attitude towards current political and social conventions is responsible for a cluster of light humorous versifiers and satirists, among them William Mackworth Praed, who is a nineteenth-century Prior in his skilful treatment of *vers de société*, and Richard Harris Barham, with his once popular *Ingoldsby Legends*; whilst C. S. Calverley, J. K. Stephen, continue with fine scholarly power the art of parody, happily inaugurated by James and Horace Smith in the famous *Rejected Addresses* so admired by one of its victims, Byron. To-day the light brigade of verse has become a regiment:

including such accomplished swordsmen as Andrew Lang, Mr. Edmund Gosse, Mr. Austin Dobson, and Mr. Owen Seaman.

A little apart from these, because of his richer fantasy and more whimsical charm, is Lewis Carroll (Charles Lutwidge Dodgson), whose unrivalled medleys, *Alice in Wonderland* and *Through the Looking-Glass*, and that delicious extravaganza, *The Hunting of the Snark*, added at once to the gaiety of the schoolroom and the library. In logical absurdities and topsy-turvy humour he has no peer save W. S. Gilbert.

Philosophic Verse.—The intellectual life and philosophic preoccupations of the mid-century find cultured expression in Sir Henry Taylor; the *Festus* of Philip James Bailey, and the *Orion* of Richard Hengist Horne. Greater than either in thought is GEORGE MEREDITH, whose lyrical vein found delightful expression in *Love in a Valley*, and *Juggling Jerry;* although in the bulk of his poems, as with Browning, it is the matter rather than the manner that counts. In other words, he thinks rather than sings in verse.

Two poets with a special vogue of their own, are EDWARD FITZGERALD and Coventry Patmore. Fitzgerald voices, with great artistic beauty and the light touch of a Horace, the sceptical thought of his day in his famous translation of *The Rubaiyát of Omar Khayyám*, which Browning essayed to answer in *Rabbi Ben Ezra*. While Patmore, standing apart both from the intellectual movement and the pre-Raphaelites, developed a gift of verse more akin to Wordsworth's than any other poet, in its simple, dignified treatment of homely themes.

2. FICTION

The extraordinary development of fiction in the eighteenth century seemed to have reached its zenith in Scott, who combined in his work the qualities of the old time romance and the realistic novel of Fielding. For a brief space the imaginative genius of the age flowed in the channels of verse. But the lull was brief. The conditions of modern life clamoured for their story-tellers, and the Victorian novel came into existence and showed what unexplored potentialities had been left undeveloped. The brilliant succession of novelists that started with Charles Dickens and closed with Thomas Hardy, left scarcely any aspect of modern existence untouched.

Middle-class ideals had found expression in eighteenth-century fiction, but meanwhile a vast class was growing up that found no articulate expression in imaginative literature. Wordsworth and Crabbe had dealt with the lives of the country poor, and Cobbett had voiced their grievances in his vigorous prose. But the London poor had no spokesman until Dickens came upon the scene. From the very start he held a brief for the humbler classes of the community, and there were few phases of struggling city life which he did not paint, very often with the pigments of personal experience. To some he is merely a popular writer of rich comic invention; to others an earnest social reformer. But neither of these pre-suppositions is sufficient to account for his persistent fame and popularity.

Charles Dickens.—He appealed, and still appeals, primarily because he deals with the large simplicities of life. He is the great story-teller of the common lives of common people; great, because, though dealing continually with little worries, little pleasures, little hardships, he made the dullest of lives in the drabbest of streets as enchanting as a fairy tale. In his hands the squalor of Lant Street becomes a fearful joy, and we would not exchange his impecunious Bohemians for all the heroes of mythology. No one shows better than he that a basic affinity with suffering lies at the root of the richest laughter. From *Pickwick* to *David Copperfield* Dickens followed, in the form of his stories, the loose picaresque methods of the elder novelists. In the manner of his satire also he owed something both to Fielding and Smollett. But his literary debts are few and slight, and he was indebted chiefly to his own genius, and to those astounding powers of observation which kept in check (sometimes with difficulty) his fantastic imagination. After *David Copperfield*, and largely through the influence of his friend Wilkie Collins, a master in the art of construction, his stories are more closely riveted together. It is questionable, however, whether the freer latitude of his earlier books did not afford more fertile scope for his splendid discursiveness. After all, he was rarely more enjoyable than when absolutely irrelevant. Who of his admirers would not exchange the elaborate plot of *Bleak House* for another Mrs. Nickleby, or the mystery behind *Edwin Drood* for the profounder mystery of Mr. Micawber's colonial experiences? But if flagging in humorous invention and easy exuberance, the later books are fully as rich in observation of London types and London sights; while in *Great Expectations* is provided a worthy companion picture to *David Copperfield*. It is drawn on a smaller scale and is set in a more subdued key. But he never did anything better in characterisation than the wholly delightful Joe Gargery and the egregious Pumblechook.

Thackeray.—His friend and contemporary, William Makepeace Thackeray, has this in common with him, that he too approaches the town life of his day from the standpoint of the humorist; there the comparison ends. As a painter of social life he is the complement, not the rival, of Dickens. Dickens deals largely with the lower middle and poorer classes of the community; Thackeray with the middle and "upper" classes. Dickens was frankly a class-man, and wrote as one who had risen from the people. He had neither the same opportunity, nor indeed the wish, for learning the ways of the richer and more exclusive circles of society. Thackeray loved good society—not from any snobbishness, but because an atmosphere of comfort and culture suited his temperament; and he is at his best in dealing with that section of society. He did for the aristocrat and clubman what Dickens did for the street vagrant and small shopkeeper—gave them a place in the pages of literature.

Thackeray's intellectual sympathies were with the late eighteenth century rather than with his own day; and his fine historical novel, *Esmond*, is less a literary experiment than a congenial expression of temperament. The title of his most popular work, *Vanity Fair*, symbolises his own attitude towards Victorian society; intensely sensitive, he often hides his real feelings, as sensitive men do, under an appearance of cynicism, but he was no cynic at heart. He is a powerful social satirist, along well-defined lines, and an accomplished though scarcely catholic literary critic. But his work as a whole, though sometimes superior in craftsmanship, lacks the splendid whimsicality and large humanity of Dickens.

Charlotte Brontë.—While Dickens and Thackeray were vitalising town life, Charlotte Brontë in her lonely northern home was finding literary outlet for the aspirations and longings of sensitive insurgent womanhood. How familiar the phrase to-day! How unfamiliar in the days when *Jane Eyre* first took the public by storm! Reserved and shy by nature, she found no means of expressing herself except with pen in hand. Then she bares her inmost thoughts and feelings. A greater contrast with the other literary daughter of a clergyman in the south it would be hard to imagine. To Jane Austen life is a comedy; it is a tragedy to Charlotte Brontë. Jane Austen's pictures are delicate water-colour miniatures; Charlotte Brontë's are oil paintings in the school of Rembrandt. Jane is severely objective in her art, detaching herself from her subject-matter. Charlotte is passionately subjective and confidential; so confidential that the reader sometimes feels as if he had overheard things not meant for utterance, but somehow forced from the writer under great stress of emotion.

As a literary artist Charlotte Brontë excels in stormy effects, whether in portraying emotional states of mind, which she renders with wonderful sincerity and subtlety, or in depicting phases of nature. What could be happier in its fine observation than the description of the Yorkshire moors—"washed from the world" in "whitening sheets of rain."

Emily Brontë.—A more remarkable personality is her sister, Emily Brontë, in whom the wildness and loneliness of the Yorkshire moors seem to become personified. Her book, *Wuthering Heights*, in sheer force of imagination is greater than anything of Charlotte's, and her verse is finer; but there is greater variety in Charlotte's work, and a more plastic art.

The Brontës' great biographer, Mrs. Gaskell, is less individual and intimate in her stories, dealing more generally with the broad social aspects of contemporary life. Especially good are her studies of life in the industrial North—notably *Mary Barton*. Her versatility is shown in such a quaint picture as *Cranford*, which reproduces the old-world charm of Miss Mitford's *Our Village*, without being in the least sense an imitation.

George Eliot.—George Eliot (Mary Ann Evans), like Tennyson, is suffering from the swing of the pendulum. Once regarded as one of our greatest novelists, her books are scarcely read at all by the present generation. And yet she is an important historic figure in the development of the English novel, with a body of work to her credit of solid lasting value.

She was the first novelist to lay the stress wholly upon character rather than on incident.

Deeply touched by the scientific influence of the age, especially by Spencer and Comte, she approached her work in quite another spirit from the Brontës. She never flung an emotional problem at her readers, but traced its source with patient acuteness, made clear to you its various confluences. She excelled in the spiritual geography of hopes, fears, and loves. Her intimate knowledge of English country life is used freely and with rich effect in her best work—in *Adam Bede*, *The Mill on the Floss*, *Silas Marner*, and *Middlemarch*. She challenges comparison here with Jane Austen, yet how different their method! Jane Austen is photographic in her fidelity, but an observer always, never a critic. One always feels the presence of the critic and the thinker in George Eliot's work. The difference will be the more readily apprehended if we compare the speeches of Miss Bates in *Emma* with those of Aunt Pullet in *The Mill on the Floss*. We can feel her amused tolerance with the foibles of her characters, hear at times her *sotto voce* comments. For tolerant she is always;

there is no novelist with a more gracious breadth of sympathy than she; while her fine sense of humour gives delightful point and freshness to her provincial settings. She served no apprenticeship to fiction; her novels show very little intellectual or artistic development. *Janet's Repentance*, in her first volume, has the freshness and insight of her best work—on a limited scale. Of all her novels, *Adam Bede* has been the most popular; but for tenderness and idyllic charm it must give place to *The Mill on the Floss*, for artistic beauty to *Silas Marner*, and for wealth of characterisation to *Middlemarch*. *Daniel Deronda* has proved a stumbling-block to many readers, and here undoubtedly the wheels of her chariot drive heavily. But a tale that contains the powerfully handled episode of Grandcourt and Gwendolen Harleth is certainly not negligible.

George Meredith.—While the literary world was vigorously applauding *Adam Bede*, *The Ordeal of Richard Feverel*, published in the same year, was passed by with scarcely any comment. George Eliot, whose acute critical faculty proved so valuable an asset to the *Westminster Review*, had been the first to extend generous recognition to the humour and imaginative charm of *The Shaving of Shagpat*; but Meredith, like Browning, was the cult of a few before he became the fashion of the many. His limited vogue is not surprising, for, despite his keen intellect and ardent imagination, his style presents often disconcerting difficulties to the average reader.

His books are best read in the light of his brilliantly suggestive *Essay on the Comic Spirit*. What makes his satire so wholesome is the fact that behind it all there is a warm poetic imagination. Severe on all superficialities of thought and feeling, he never mocks at true romance. There is one noble sentence of his that strikes the keynote of all his psychology: "You may estimate your capacity for comic perception by being able to detect the ridicule of them you love without loving them less." And so far as his philosophy of life can be put into a phrase, it is here: "We do not get to any heaven by renouncing the mother we sprang from; and when there is an eternal secret for us, it is best to believe that Earth knows, to keep near her even in our utmost aspiration."

Contemporary with George Eliot and the early years of Meredith is Anthony Trollope, a writer of immense popularity in his time. Without the genius of the great Victorians, he showed himself to be a craftsman of great ability, and in the Barsetshire novels he has given us a picture of English provincial life in a cathedral town, remarkable for shrewd observation of character and a lively if not very subtle humour. One illustrious character at least he added to the gallery of the immortals of fiction, the awe-inspiring Mrs. Proudie.

The last great Victorian novelist, however, is Mr. THOMAS HARDY, who in his later years has returned to verse writing. Interesting and vital as his poetry is, it is as a story-teller of life in the south-west of England that he will be best remembered.

Deriving to some extent from George Eliot, and from the work of the French Realistic school, his fiction bears the distinctive impress of an original and highly sensitive mind. Lacking the intellectual vigour and plasticity of Meredith, he is an incomparably better story-teller, with a spacious, deliberate manner, and a rare insight into simple, uncultured, elemental natures. He has little interest in the jostling crowds of the city which attracted Dickens and Thackeray, or for the complexities of man as a civilised animal, which fascinated Meredith. To depict the primal things of life ; to dally with old-world customs ; to paint men and women as the inevitable outcome of a certain environment, that was the aim of Hardy. He is a dweller in Arcadia, but not the Arcadia of Wordsworth and Scott. There is nothing of Rousseau's idealism in his pictures of nature ; rather is it the tragedies and ironies of country life upon which he elects to dwell; though in his earlier books—*e.g. Under the Greenwood Tree*, and *Far from the Madding Crowd*—these are lightened by a delightful humour. His excessive sensitiveness to the "still sad music of humanity" imparts a depressing atmosphere to many of his later novels. But there can be little doubt that he will take his place among our greatest novelists by virtue of the high artistic beauty of his best work, and his consummate power of actualising subtle impressions and fleeting moods.

The last characteristic finds an exponent of quite another temperament in Mr. Henry James ; but Mr. James expends his subtle psychology chiefly upon the cultured classes. Two other psychological novelists of distinction are John Oliver Hobbes (Mrs. Craigie) and Mrs. Humphry Ward. The first has a Gallic wit and sense of style denied to her contemporary ; but Mrs. Ward's work has more solid qualities, and she has given us some thoughtful and vigorous pictures of modern English life and thought. To-day the character novel is leavened with sociology, as in the work of that versatile writer Mr. H. G. Wells.

The realistic school, that had so remarkable a vogue in France, headed by Zola, has found no very secure place in English literature, though it has influenced some of our story-tellers. Mr. George Moore is the ablest of the English "realists," and his *Mummer's Wife* and *Esther Waters* are among the best of their kind.

Less powerful, but none the less faithful presentations of phases of middle-class lives are the stories of George Gissing. He was a fine man of letters, rarely able to do justice to his artistic power.

Turning now from the character novel to the story of incident, we find ourselves in the midst of a multitude of writers from whom it is possible only to select a few representative names. Incident pure and simple such as we find in earlier fiction, the military stories of Charles Lever and the naval yarns of Marryat, are rare in Victorian times. Even born romancers like Charles Kingsley are drawn for a while into the social vortex of the hour. Agricultural problems are set forth in *Yeast;* industrial defects in *Alton Locke.* But his picturesque pen finds greater artistic scope in the patriotic romance of *Westward Ho,* in the tale of the break-up of the Roman Empire, *Hypatia,* and in the invigorating fantasy for children, *The Water Babies.* Similar in his gifts, and in the opinion of many, a better story-teller, was his brother Henry Kingsley, whose *Ravenshoe* retains its popularity even to-day.

With a large measure of Charles Kingsley's lively imagination, something also of his inequality as an artist, is Charles Reade. Starting as a writer of plays, he rarely forgot the limelight when he turned to fiction; but he had, at his best, in common with his greater contemporary Dickens, dramatic power and intensity of a high order. This it is which makes the reader forget at times the inordinate length of *The Cloister and the Hearth*—an historical romance of splendid episodic force—and gives colour and interest to *It's Never too Late to Mend, Foul Play,* and *Hard Cash,* where the story-teller exhibits in turn prison abuses, convict life in Australia, and the treatment of the insane. With many of the gifts of the romancer Reade combined enormous industry in getting up his case, and an indomitable humanitarian zeal. His friend Wilkie Collins, in his social sympathies resembled Reade, but his abilities as a writer ran in directions apart from the novel with a purpose. Of all Victorian novelists he is perhaps the most neglected to-day, yet he is, as a weaver of complicated plots, unequalled among English writers. He had what his French rival, Gaboriau, mostly lacked, a real sense of character. In his best books, *The Woman in White, After Dark, The Moonstone, Armadale,* and *No Name,* he shows imaginative power of a high order.

Another type of novelist who romanticised the less familiar

actualities of ordinary life, is illustrated by George Borrow. His knowledge of gipsy life, which his peculiar temperament gave him unusual opportunities of studying, imparts a distinctive flavour to his attractive vagrant stories, *Lavengro*, *The Romany Rye*, and *The Bible in Spain*. As agent for the Bible Society he had opportunities for travel which afforded him rich material for his tales. These are, in the main, imaginative autobiographies. Another writer who made the gipsy a live thing in fiction is the poet and critic Mr. Watts-Dunton, whose *Aylwin* is at once a fine discursive romance and an interesting picture of contemporary literary life.

Honest, straightforward romancers with a good story to tell were William Black and Sir Walter Besant, while on a higher imaginative plane is R. D. Blackmore; and the name of J. H. Shorthouse is associated with one striking historical novel, *John Inglesant*.

Among the crowd of story-tellers who kept, like Wilkie Collins, more to everyday life with judicious seasoning of melodrama, the familiar names of Miss Braddon and Mrs. Henry Wood detach themselves readily. Turgid and artificial in her pictures of "high life," but with real though undisciplined imagination, is the prolific and once widely read "Ouida."

In George MacDonald we have a healthy Scottish novelist of no special distinction, and a Gaelic romancer with a touch of genius, whose fantasies for children have never been rivalled save by the incomparable Hans Andersen. *On the Back of the North Wind*, *The Princess and the Goblin*, and *Phantasies*, are among the very best of their kind. Mrs. Oliphant, a prolific and versatile writer, and contributor to *Blackwood's Magazine*, touched at times a high level of excellence—notably in *The Beleaguered City*.

Three names claiming more special attention are ROBERT LOUIS STEVENSON, whose piquant blend of humour and imaginative exuberance finds characteristic expression in *The New Arabian Nights*; William Morris, who fashioned his Utopian dreams from the best elements of mediævalism; and the earlier Rudyard Kipling, who gave his realistic pictures of Anglo-Indian life a fascinating background of oriental mystery. Both Stevenson and Morris were stylists of a high order who did much for the beautifying of English prose. Morris, however, deliberately eschewed humour in his romances, and both Stevenson and Kipling achieve some of their most characteristic effects by means of it. There is a good deal of the eternal child in both Stevenson and Morris. Stevenson approached romance much in the mood of the "young man with the cream tarts"; while the gusto and high spirits of *Treasure Island* are readily communicated to the reader. Morris's frank delight in the healthy actualities and the wistful idealism of youth untouched by the preoccupation of the civilised man is one of the chief charms of such fascinating literature as *The Dream of John Ball* and *The Wood beyond the World*. His frank, pagan love of the earth and its beauty finds a counterpart in the rhythmic prose of Richard Jefferies, whose *Life of the Fields*, and pictures of country sights and sounds in Southern England, are in literary descent from Gilbert White's *Selborne*, and claim imaginative affinity with Thoreau's *Walden*.

Morris's romances, like his poetry, are something apart from the trend of Victorian fiction. Stevenson, however, found successors on the historical side in Mr. Quiller Couch, Mr. Anthony Hope, and Mr. Stanley Weyman, to mention a few of the most notable; while Mr. Maurice Hewlett certainly derives from him in part.

3. History and Criticism

The work of THOMAS CARLYLE belongs only in part to the Victorian Era, but with the exception of *Sartor Resartus* his most characteristic work was published during that time. *The French Revolution* appeared in 1837, and 1865 saw the intrepid veteran emerging from what Mrs. Carlyle humorously and not unfittingly called "The Valley of the Shadow of Frederic." During the early years of struggle at Ecclefechan he did much to familiarise English readers with German literature. But his first characteristic utterance is *Sartor Resartus*, where his emphatic but negative gospel may be found. It is in essence a tilt against shams of every kind, expressed in the form of an assumed record about Teufelsdröckh and his "philosophy of clothes,"—a notion borrowed from Swift. *The French Revolution* which followed was in itself a revolution in the making of a history. In form only is it a prose history; in essence it is a poetic rhapsody on the elemental forces that make for social disintegration. The book made his name, though not his fortune. Later came *Heroes and Hero Worship*, from which emerged definitely his admiration of might—wherever he found it; and the tendency to associate might with right, which led him to bestow the aureole, at times, on some sorry saints.

Among Carlyle's miscellaneous and political essays none struck a fresher note than the well-known eulogy of the Middle Ages in *Past and Present*, while his work on Cromwell is the finest piece of effective special pleading for puritanism that we have. As a stylist he reminds us of his propinquity with the romantic movement. It is prose in revolt against eighteenth-century canons; prose as idiosyncratic as that of Hazlitt and Lamb. Violent and chaotic often, it is amazingly vivid and ardent; with a grim and savage grandeur at times that takes the reader by the throat.

The humorist in Carlyle must not be overlooked. He is not a genial humorist like Dickens, or a whimsical one like Lamb, but a trenchant sardonic one, and this gives a sharp relish to the abundance of luminous criticism which his writings contain. For all his pæan on brute force, and the harsh impatience which animates many of his social strictures, he had a strain of deep tenderness in his nature, and if "gey ill to live wi'," was a loyal friend, and at bottom a great-hearted man.

History in Carlyle's view was—Biography writ large. The great man made the age. The opposite view was expressed by his contemporary Buckle. If Carlyle was too little affected by the scientific ideas of his time, Buckle no doubt generalised too hastily; but for all the exaggeration, his unfinished *History of Civilisation*—in which the thesis that environment makes the age, and the great man too—is full of fruitful suggestions. In his power of actualising history, Carlyle has no mean rival in Thomas Babington Macaulay. Gifted with a prodigious memory, scholarly tastes, splendid industry, and great power of mental assimilation, he had at his command a vast array of literary and historical allusions that imparted point and lucidity to his pictures. For he would give to a social vignette all the vividness and reality of a novel, and had the lawyer's power of condensing and clarifying an intricate subject. In this he excels Carlyle, just as he falls below him in deep imaginative power.

Another great proseman of the period is Carlyle's biographer, James Anthony Froude. As an historian he has been much criticised for his lack of accuracy. Notwithstanding this admitted defect, he has, quite as fully as Carlyle and Macaulay, the power of making the dry bones of history live. Added to this he has a literary style, less fatiguing than Carlyle's, and with nothing of that hard metallic glitter which wearies one often in the Whig historian. His *History of England from the Fall of Wolsey to the Defeat of the Armada* has done more to make Englishmen realise the characteristics of that age than any other work. Not all his writing was equally good, but his *Bunyan* is excellent, and for cultured thought and grace of style his *Short Studies* must be put in the front rank of his writings. E. A. Freeman, his most hostile critic, did admirable work as a specialist in certain fields of history—*e.g.* The Norman Conquest, but his pugnacity often warped his judgment.

Of greater literary interest is the work of Freeman's pupil, John Richard Green, whose lively and scholarly imagination and picturesque style made of the *Short History of the English People* one of the best introductions to our history in the language.

The name of Henry Hallam will always be connected with the first serious attempt to treat history in a more impartial and unprejudiced manner; if not a great writer, he was eminently fair-minded, and the modern school of historians are certainly indebted to him. Among the modern school, including many names of distinction, are W. E. H. Lecky, the scholarly historian of the eighteenth century and of *European Morals;* James Bryce, with his searching picture of *The Holy Roman Empire* and his monumental *American Commonwealth;* James Gardiner, who did in substance for the early Stuarts and Cromwell what Froude did for the Tudors, with greater impartiality of method if with less charm of style; Mandell Creighton; Gairdner, and Bishop Stubbs—learned and well-balanced writers in ecclesiastical and mediæval history; and Professor Seeley, a most stimulating and suggestive historical critic.

Turning from history to more distinctively critical work, there is Matthew Arnold, whose *Essays in Criticism* proved highly suggestive, less as actual criticisms of various writers than as a guide to a *method* of appreciation. These should be read in connection with the more valuable *Culture and Anarchy*, embodying Arnold's educational ideas, and indicating some greatly needed criticism of English ways of thought. Arnold's ideal of culture may be compared and considered advantageously with T. H. Huxley's *Educational Essays.* Fundamentally they are not at variance, but present the problem from the different points of view of the scholar-poet and the cultured man of science. Huxley is one of the few scientists with a vigorous vital style, by means of which he did much to popularise the ideas of Spencer and Darwin, and to apply them to current religious and social ideals.

A gifted and versatile man of letters is George Henry Lewes, whose encouragement of George Eliot was distinctly valuable, and who touched with airy grace, philosophy, biography, fiction, and criticism. His best work is his *Life of Goethe.*

Meanwhile theology as well as science is productive of some

considerable literary forces. In the conservative wing there is John Henry Newman, a skilful and accomplished dialectician and a stylist of singular beauty. This is exhibited in his famous *Apologia* (called forth by Kingsley's attack); even more in the *Plain and Parochial Sermons*. The Tractarian Movement, with its insistence on culture, can claim several notable figures. We have the pellucid piety of Keble's verse, the fine critical judgment of Dean Church, and the ripe culture of Mark Pattison. The Broad Church party gives us that picturesque historian, Dean Stanley; and that somewhat enigmatic personality, Jowett; Frederick Denison Maurice, pioneer of Christian Socialism, and Robertson of Brighton, whose working-class lectures on poetry were singularly fresh and attractive. On the radical side there are Francis Newman with his vigorously outspoken *Phases of Faith;* W. R. Greg, a trenchant critic of social and religious problems, and greatest of all intellectually and spiritually, the Unitarian James Martineau. As a stylist Martineau inclines rather to the rich eloquence of the Jacobean prose-man. His earlier work sometimes is overladen with ornament; but in *Hours of Thought*, and *The Seat of Authority in Religion*, the style is chastened, and for sheer beauty of thought and expression no other prose of our time can rival it.

His sister Harriet achieved less distinction but wider popularity for her vigorous criticisms on social politics.

As a dominating personality in the public eye, there is only one name, however, which for range of influence is comparable with Carlyle's, and that is Carlyle's friend, to some extent his follower, JOHN RUSKIN. Fundamentally they had much in common. Each stood aloof from the political and social life of his age, calling down curses with cheerful impartiality on both great parties. Both of them were sturdily Puritan at heart, and out of touch with many of the manifestations of modern civilisation. Both, moreover, aimed at social reconstruction.

As literary forces, there was much to differentiate them. Carlyle's style is rough and staccato; Ruskin's rhythmic and legato. Carlyle dramatised his subject: Ruskin presents it like a diorama before us. Carlyle was a literary pioneer, in the first place, making Goethe known to us. Ruskin was an art pioneer, the spokesman for Turner. Both are social critics, but whereas Carlyle was a social as well as literary critic from the first, it was late in life before Ruskin turned from Art Reform to Social Reform.

Ruskin did a great work in bringing the plastic Arts and

the Master Art of Architecture before the general reader. The relation between Art and Nature, the imaginative and ethical influence of great Art, was expatiated upon by Ruskin in *Modern Painters, The Seven Lamps of Architecture*, and *Stones of Venice*, with all the illustrative eloquence his style could give it. In form his style is of the seventeenth century; it owes much to the splendid rhetoric of the Old Testament, and although too self-conscious and over ornate at times, is finely adapted for its special purpose—*i.e.* to stimulate the conscience and imagination of the reader. His later writings from *Unto this Last* (which made as much stir as Carlyle's *Sartor Resartus*), to the autobiography *Fors Clavigera* deal entirely with economic and educational subjects, in which he advocates what is best described as an aristocratic type of Socialism, as contrasted with the democratic type favoured by his follower William Morris. A feature of his later work is the liberal use of irony, which scarcely ever touches his earlier writings.

Two critics who derive in style from Ruskin are, John Addington Symonds, with his eloquent *Renaissance in Italy*, and Walter Pater, whose fastidious literary palate and artistic sympathies, found expression in a small body of essays, notably *Appreciations*, and a story of the second century, *Marius the Epicurean*, which is less a novel than an exposition of Pater's life-philosophy—coterminous with Keats' "Beauty is Truth, Truth Beauty."

Oscar Wilde.—Another who came for a time under Ruskin's influence was that brilliant Irishman, Oscar Wilde; but the influence was æsthetic rather than intellectual. Wilde, like his fellow-countryman, Mr. Bernard Shaw, set about to disturb the complacency of the middle-class Saxon, in matters of art and letters. He succeeded so well by virtue of his wilful Irish wit and frank self-advertising, that the majority of people even to-day regard him as little better than a *poseur* with a gift for superficial paradox.

That he did pose outrageously, and *did* indulge in much that was merely cheap and flashy, cannot be gainsaid. But he was much more than this. At his best he was an artist of no little genius. His *Soul of Man under Socialism* is a fine piece of analytical criticism; and his literary palate was as delicate and sure as Pater's—witness that admirable volume on Art and Literature: *Intentions*. He had little creative imagination. One cannot imagine *Dorian Gray* existing had there been no Balzac and Gautier; and his verse takes on, chameleon-like, the colour of the poet he has last been reading; whilst even such a charming fantasy as the *Happy Prince* is a brilliant experiment in Hans Andersen's manner. But he had a subtle sense of style, which he used with splendid effect in *De Profundis*; and he was above all a wit of rare quality. This it is which gives peculiar value to his critical estimates, and combined with his sense of the theatre, enabled him to write one supremely exquisite comedy, *The Importance of being Earnest.*

Among other critics whose work is less impressionistic, more analytical in method than those mentioned, are Walter Bagehot, an economist of note and a literary critic of restricted but unquestionable power; Richard Holt Hutton of *The Spectator*, and Professor Edward Dowden excelling notably in ethical estimates; Mr. Edmund Gosse and Mr. Stopford Brooke especially admirable in poetical estimates; Professor Saintsbury, of encyclopædic knowledge; Mr. Frederic Harrison, the exponent of Comte's Philosophy, and that great journalist and distinguished writer, Lord Morley. Finally, there is Mr. Watts-Dunton, who during the mid-century made *The Athenæum* a living force in the world of letters with his versatile and cultured pen.

Modern Industrial and Economic problems have attracted many minds to-day. A few representative names are Mr. Edward Carpenter, the poet of modern democracy; Mr. and Mrs. Sidney Webb, its accomplished historians; Samuel Butler, author of *Erewhon*, its satirist; and Mr. Belfort Bax, Mr. J. A. Hobson, and Mr. Bernard Shaw among its ablest sociological critics.

4. A Note on Present-day Tendencies

About fifteen years before the death of Queen Victoria the familiar landmarks of the Victorian Era began to crumble away, and a transitional period followed from which we have not yet emerged.

Two features detach themselves from the crowd of jostling forces, as especially remarkable: the far-reaching influence of modern Journalism, and the revival of the Drama.

The newspaper of to-day has influenced literature both for good and ill. At its worst, it has encouraged superficiality in life and letters, has mistaken smartness for brilliance, and mere sensationalism for imaginative power; at its best, it has banished prolixity and artificiality, and made for clearness, conciseness, and reality.

Its effect upon Poetry can be gauged by a glance at Mr. Kipling's verse. Deficient often in dignity and beauty, it is amazingly alive and actual; and from the *Barrack Room Ballads*, through the work of W. E. Henley and John Davidson, to

Mr. Masefield's *Widow of Bye Street*; this alert, tingling vitality has been the prominent feature of our most characteristic latter-day verse.

The second characteristic of to-day is certainly the renascence of the drama. This is clearly connected with the dominance of journalism, inasmuch as the desire to appeal instantly and directly makes the art form of the drama a more favourable medium of expression than either verse or fiction.

From the nineties of the last century, when Oscar Wilde enlivened the stage as none since Sheridan had done, to the intellectual nimbleness of Mr. Bernard Shaw, and the mystical beauty of the work of J. M. Synge, some of the most energising personalities of the day have elected for the theatre as their base of operations. Nor has this been confined to England. The revival of the Drama has taken place all over Europe, and what Ibsen did for his countrymen, Mr. Bernard Shaw and his followers have done for the English Drama. They have torn away from the stage the conventional sentimentalism and unrealities that had made Victorian drama so largely negligible and have helped to make it a force in social life, as potent almost as was the Victorian novel.

From the artistic standpoint, most forms of literature to-day are passing through a transitional, experimental stage. Freshness is esteemed more than form and beauty. A few of our writers, Mr. W. B. Yeats for example, are fine artists: but more are content to speak to their generation as journalists rather than as men of letters. This is not to imply that Journalism is inferior literature; but merely that it is something other than literature. It works on a different plane, with methods of its own. Journalism is essentially impressionistic, aims at an instant appeal, and is content with arousing interest and provoking thought. In an Age of increasing hurry and bustle, Journalism has a great and important work to do. Only it is not the work of literature. Literature is less omnivorous and comprehensive than Journalism. It is selective, eclectic, and while it needs freshness and reality to keep it sweet and wholesome, it needs also beauty of form and a high seriousness of treatment (which by no means excludes humour) to give it durability.

The defect of the literature of to-day, taken as a whole, is to confuse these divergent ideals. This, however, is a tendency peculiar to transitional periods. And one thing, at any rate, we realise clearly enough, that only those portions of our national literature which have in them the living human element, will be allowed to survive by that most searching of all critics—Time.

HINTS FOR FURTHER STUDY

THE most compendious study for the student is Saintsbury's *Short History of English Literature.* (Macmillan, 7s. 6d. net.) This may be supplemented by Chambers's *Cyclopedia of English Literature.* (Published in sixpenny parts.)

An invaluable reference is the *Dictionary of National Biography.*

For the EARLIER PERIOD.—Stopford Brooke's *History of Early English Literature;* Hale's *Age of Chaucer.* (George Bell, 3s. 6d.) Carlyle's *Past and Present* gives a vivid picture of mediæval monastic life. Jusserand's *Literary History of the English People,* vol. i. (Fisher Unwin) contains admirable studies of William Langland and Chaucer. Langland's *Piers the Plowman* (school edition), edited by Prof. Skeat. (Clarendon Press.) Among the best short critical studies of Chaucer are—Hazlitt's lecture in *Lectures on the English Poets* (Bohn), and Lowell's essay on Chaucer in *My Study Windows* (Houghton). Modernised versions of *The Canterbury Tales* are given in the "King's Classics" (De La More Press, 2s. 6d.), by Prof. Skeat. *Popular Studies in Mythology, Romance, and Folklore* (David Nutt, 6d. each), should be read for a clear and concise record of mediæval romance (Arthurian cycle, &c.).

For the period of the ENGLISH RENASCENCE.—Symond's art. "Renaissance," in the *Encyclopædia Britannica;* Jusserand's *Literary History of the English People* (vols. ii. and iii.); Goadby's *The England of Shakespeare* (Cassell); Hazlitt's *Lectures on the Dramatic Literature of the Age of Elizabeth;* Symond's *Shakespeare's Predecessors in the English Drama;* Dowden's *Shakespeare: his Mind and Art* (Paul Trench). The Mermaid Series (*Best Plays of the Old Dramatists,* 2s. 6d. each). Biographies of Milton, Spenser, and Bunyan in "English Men of Letters" Series (Macmillan).

For the AGE OF DRYDEN, POPE, AND JOHNSON.—Garnett's *Age of Dryden;* Dennis's *Age of Pope.* (Macmillan, 3s. 6d.) Biographies of Dryden, Addison, Pope and Johnson, Defoe, Richardson, Fielding, Sterne, in "English Men of Letters" Series. Hazlitt's *Lectures on the English Poets;* Macaulay's essay on *Dryden;* Lamb's essay on *The Artificial Comedy of the Last Century;* Leslie Stephen's *Defoe's Novels* (Hours in a Library).

For the NINETEENTH CENTURY LITERATURE.—Saintsbury's *History of Nineteenth Century Literature.* (Macmillan, 7s. 6d.) Herford's *Age of Wordsworth;* Walker's *Age of Tennyson.* (Macmillan, 3s. 6d.) The "English Men of Letters" Series (Wordsworth, Shelley, Keats, Byron, Carlyle, Lamb, George Eliot, Matthew Arnold, Rossetti). George Gissing's "Charles Dickens"; Chesterton's "Dickens." Admirable Studies of Tennyson and Browning by Stopford Brooke. Brief and cheap studies of William Morris by Prof. Mackail and Holbrook Jackson. For the development of modern fiction, Raleigh's *English Novel.* For the social aspect of the literary life of the age, see *The London Life of Yesterday* (Constable).